"I am so thankful for Ed Drew and his commitment to lifting Jesus up for our children. *Meals With Jesus* has done the heavy lifting in shaping questions and conversations that meet families where they are. I'll be going through it with my kids! Thank you for this bright, thoughtful, engaging and much-needed tool for families to remember our great Lord and Savior together."

RANDALL GOODGAME, Slugs & Bugs Family Music

"If you struggle to read the Bible regularly with your children (and who doesn't?), this is a great resource. Imaginative and easy to use, whatever age and stage your children are, this study in Luke's Gospel is full of practical ideas, wise insights and some great applications."

TREVOR ARCHER, London Director, FIEC; father of four, grandad to seven

"Ed Drew takes families on a wonderful journey through Luke's Gospel, exploring who Jesus is through the various meals Jesus shared. The most important thing a parent can do for their child is to show them Jesus. This book helps every parent to do just that. Ed has a wonderful way of giving parents fresh language that's age appropriate and beautifully rich yet simple and clear. Every family, whatever their shape or size, will find this resource accessible and easy to use. And every family who embarks on this journey will be blessed by it."

SANDY GALEA, MBM Kids' Ministry Director; Founder, Kidswise

"Would you like to have to Jesus join you for a family meal? Well, here's the next best thing—a series of simple Bible studies through which your children can meet Jesus around the dinner table. *Meals with Jesus* includes something for every member of the family, with a focus on how the good news speaks to our hearts."

TIM CHESTER, Pastor, Grace Church, Boroughbridge; Faculty Member, Crossland Training

"This book is a feast for each family member. Taste and see the goodness of Jesus Christ in Ed's short Bible readings and probing age-appropriate questions, while together you grow a deeper delight in our Savior. Parents, if you are looking to be spiritually fed yourselves while training your children to glorify Jesus, this book is for you."

CHERYCE BERG, Director of Children's Ministries, College Church, Wheaton

Ed Drew

Meals with Jesus

A journey through Luke's Gospel
for the whole family

Meals with Jesus
© Faith in Kids 2021
www.faithinkids.org

Published by:
The Good Book Company

thegoodbook.com | thegoodbook.co.uk
thegoodbook.com.au | thegoodbook.co.nz | thegoodbook.co.in

ISBN: 9781784985769 | Printed in India

Cover and design by André Parker | Illustrations by Isobel Lundie

Contents

Before you begin

Welcome to *Meals with Jesus*, a journey through Luke's Gospel for the whole family.

Christians are not primarily about an institution, a religion, a habit or a set of behaviours. We are about Jesus Christ. As we sit with him at the dinner table, we see who he is: his decision-making, his compassion and his bravery. When we sit with him, we meet the man we spend so long talking about. As we look him square in the eye, we get the chance to make the biggest decisions of our lives. What do we think of him? Do we like him? Do we trust him? Will we dare to follow him?

There will come a day, if it has not already happened, when our sons and daughters will not take our word for it. They won't just do what their parents did before them. They need to hear it for themselves—the whole story—so that they can make their own decisions. With these studies your family will have the chance to look Jesus in the eye, to ask their deepest questions and to hear him speaking to them.

Come and have a meal with Jesus.

HOW TO READ THESE STORIES DURING LENT

	MON	TUE	WED	THU	FRI	SAT	SUN
WK 1		Shrove Tuesday Pancakes!	Day 1 Lk 5 v 27-28	Day 2 Lk 5 v 29-30	Day 3 Lk 5 v 31-32		
WK 2	Day 4 Lk 5 v 31-32	Day 5 Lk 7 v 36-39	Day 6 Lk 7 v 40-43	Day 7 Lk 7 v 44-50	Day 8 Lk 7 v 37-38, 47-48		
WK 3	Day 9 Lk 9 v 10-11	Day 10 Lk 9 v 12-14	Day 11 Lk 9 v 15-17	Day 12 Lk 9 v 16-17	Day 13 Lk 10 v 38-42		
WK 4	Day 14 Lk 10 v 38-42	Day 15 Lk 6 v 46-49	Day 16 Lk 10 v 41-42	Day 17 Lk 14 v 1-6	Day 18 Lk 14 v 7-11		
WK 5	Day 19 Lk 14 v 12-14	Day 20 Lk 14 v 11	Day 21 Lk 19 v 1-4	Day 22 Lk 19 v 5-7	Day 23 Lk 19 v 8-10		
WK 6	Day 24 Lk 19 v 5-10	Day 25 Lk 22 v 7-16	Day 26 Lk 22 v 17-23	Day 27 Lk 22 v 24-27	Day 28 Lk 22 v 15-20		
WK 7	Day 29 Lk 24 v 13-24	Day 30 Lk 24 v 25-29	Day 31 Lk 24 v 30-35	Day 32 Lk 24 v 30-34	Day 33 Good Friday Lk 14 v 15-20		Day 34 Easter Sunday Lk 14 v 21-24

Note: On both charts, the **"hit the heart" stories** are the ones with a grey background.

HOW TO ENJOY THESE STORIES AT ANY TIME OF YEAR

	MEAL	THEME	DAY 1	DAY 2	DAY 3	DAY 4
WK 1	Lunch with Levi	The joy of following	**Day 1** Lk 5 v 27-28	**Day 2** Lk 5 v 29-30	**Day 3** Lk 5 v 31-32	**Day 4** Lk 5 v 31-32
WK 2	Simon's show	Gratitude for forgiveness	**Day 5** Lk 7 v 36-39	**Day 6** Lk 7 v 40-43	**Day 7** Lk 7 v 44-50	**Day 8** Lk 7 v 37-38, 47-48
WK 3	Mega picnic	Contentment from knowing we have all we need	**Day 9** Lk 9 v 10-11	**Day 10** Lk 9 v 12-14	**Day 11** Lk 9 v 15-17	**Day 12** Lk 9 v 16-17
WK 4	At Mary and Martha's	We delight to hear Jesus speak	**Day 13** Lk 10 v 38-42	**Day 14** Lk 10 v 38-42	**Day 15** Lk 6 v 46-49	**Day 16** Lk 10 v 41-42
WK 5	Best seat in the house	The humility to put others first	**Day 17** Lk 14 v 1-6	**Day 18** Lk 14 v 7-11	**Day 19** Lk 14 v 12-14	**Day 20** Lk 14 v 11
WK 6	At home with Zach	Amazement that Jesus came for the worst	**Day 21** Lk 19 v 1-4	**Day 22** Lk 19 v 5-7	**Day 23** Lk 19 v 8-10	**Day 24** Lk 19 v 5-10
WK 7	The last supper	Awestruck that Jesus died to take us to the final feast	**Day 25** Lk 22 v 7-16	**Day 26** Lk 22 v 17-23	**Day 27** Lk 22 v 24-27	**Day 28** Lk 22 v 15-20
WK 8	Supper in Emmaus	Sure hope because of Jesus' resurrection	**Day 29** Lk 24 v 13-24	**Day 30** Lk 24 v 25-29	**Day 31** Lk 24 v 30-35	**Day 32** Lk 24 v 30-34
WK 9	Invite to the banquet	Who will be at the final meal with Jesus?	**Day 33** Lk 14 v 15-20	**Day 34** Lk 14 v 21-24		

WHAT YOU CAN EXPECT

Take ten minutes with your family each day.

Whether you have a child of three or eighteen, this flexible, easy-to-use resource will allow the whole family to celebrate a month of meals with Jesus.

The devotions we've created aim to be an achievable joy, not an unrealistic burden. No more than ten minutes are needed to complete a daily section. If you want to take longer, that's great!

We spend three days exploring each meal, followed by a "hit the heart" day to draw the themes of that meal together and apply them to our hearts.

There are two charts on pages 8-9. One shows you how to use these stories during Lent, as you build up to the Easter weekend. The other shows how you can use them at any time of year, on four days per week. Choose whichever approach works best for your family.

And if you'd like a bit more help, any tricky questions include an example answer in brackets after the question. There are also some top tips on page 123 at the back of the book.

I am so grateful to Tim Chester for his book *A Meal with Jesus*, which inspired, encouraged and advised me as I wrote these studies for my family and yours.

DAY 1

Leaving it all behind

Where are we going today?

Jesus picked a hated tax collector to become his friend. Levi left everything to follow Jesus.

READY?

- **Optional.** Can each person grab two or three objects that are precious to them or that represent favourite activities? Parents might grab a purse, a family picture or their car keys. Children might grab a soft toy, a screen, a photo of a friend, a soccer ball or a favourite piece of clothing.

- Open your Bible to **Luke 5 v 27-28** (or read the passage from page 12).

LET'S GO!

Pray: Dear Father, help us to understand what is most precious. Amen.

Perhaps try...

- Lay out your precious items on the floor.

- What emergency would it take for you to run out of your home right now and leave them *all* behind?

- If you can't do this activity, ask a quick question instead: Which object is most precious to you?

- *Link: In today's story Levi left everything to follow Jesus.*

This week's story

- *Where are we in the Bible?* Jesus has begun to cause a stir. News is spreading about him. Crowds have been gathering. Now it is time for Jesus to choose a group of friends to be his disciples.

- *Look out for* what we are told about the man Jesus chooses. (Look at the box on page 13 for more about tax collectors.)

- *Read* the passage.

Luke 5 v 27-28

²⁷ *After this, Jesus went out and saw a tax collector named Levi sitting in the tax office. Jesus said to him, "Follow me!"* ²⁸ *Levi got up, left everything, and followed Jesus.*

Questions for us all

1. What do you think a tax collector would have on his desk? *(If you want, you could put your wallet, phone and house keys out in front of you.)*

2. What sort of things do you imagine would fill Levi's normal working day?

Question for 3s and 4s

What did Levi do when Jesus said, "Follow me"?

Question for 5-7s

What did Levi take with him, as he went to follow Jesus?

Question for over-7s

Why would Levi or you leave everything to follow someone?

Question for teens

You make choices each day about who to follow, who to be with, who to listen to, who to imitate… How do you make those decisions? What is it about Jesus that has attracted you to following him? OR What would Jesus need to be like for you or your friends to choose to follow him?

Think and pray

Thank Jesus for the good things he has given you. Have you discovered what you value more than Jesus? Talk to him about that.

Got time to chat?

What and who we value leads quickly to the decisions we make. Think about how you choose to fill your spare time, which people you choose to be around, and who you wish you could see more often. Can you see from these decisions what you value, what you love, who you trust, and how you choose friends? Levi saw in Jesus all that he valued, all that he needed, and exactly who he needed to listen to.

Something more for the adults?

We know the tax collector Levi better as Matthew, the writer of the first Gospel. It's intriguing that Matthew chose not to write about his own calling in his Gospel, but instead he tells us about his friends being called to follow Jesus. Read Matthew 4 v 18-22. Matthew must have smiled as he wrote this and remembered his own story. What do we learn about discipleship from these passages? Before you load a burden on yourself to be more, to think more, or to do more, just take a moment to ponder what we learn about Jesus' role in discipleship.

A note about tax collectors

Levi was a tax collector: a Jew working for the Roman Empire. The Roman Empire had invaded the Jewish country, had made life harder for the Jewish people, and had killed some of Levi's own people. So the Jewish people hated the Roman Empire for taking away their freedom. This meant that Levi and other tax collectors were hated traitors. They were collecting money from their own people to give to the Roman Empire; that money paid for the hated Roman soldiers to stay in their country!

It gets even worse. The tax collectors could charge whatever they liked. So if Levi's Jewish neighbour owed two denarii, he could charge them three or four denarii and keep the extra money. Tax collectors got rich by stealing money from their own people. And if anyone argued, the Roman soldiers were on hand. Can you imagine how much the Jewish people hated Levi and the other tax collectors?

Jesus chose Levi! No one else chose to even talk to Levi. But Jesus went back to Levi's for a party. Why? Did Jesus know what Levi had done?

DAY 2
The strangest party

Where are we going today?

Jesus chose to go home with the worst of people for a party with other scumbags.

READY?

- **Optional.** Collect a few objects for each member of the family, to represent people. Some toy characters? Or just some big spoons?

- Open up your Bible to **Luke 5 v 29-30** (or read the passage from page 15).

LET'S GO!

Pray: Dear Father, please help us to understand why Jesus chose to make friends with mean people. Amen.

Perhaps try...

- Each person picks two of their best friends. Tell each other about them. Why do you like them?

- Now imagine totally opposite people. Use the objects you've collected to represent these imaginary people. So, if your friend loves playing with you, imagine someone who only spoils your games and shouts at you. If your friend is kind, imagine someone selfish and mean. Let's give these imaginary anti-friends names such as Mean Milly or Angry Alan.

- If you can't do this activity, ask a quick question instead: Describe someone you would never want as a friend.

- *Link: How would it feel walking into a party of those people? That is exactly where Jesus goes in today's story.*

This week's story

- *Where are we in the Bible?* Jesus walked up to Levi and told him, "Follow me". Where did they go next?
- *Look out for* what the Jewish leaders were angry about.
- *Read* the passage.

Luke 5 v 29-30

²⁹ Then Levi gave a big dinner for Jesus. The dinner was at Levi's house. At the table there were many tax collectors and other people, too. ³⁰ But the Pharisees and the men who taught the law for the Pharisees began to complain to the followers of Jesus. They said, "Why do you eat and drink with tax collectors and 'sinners'?"

Questions for us all

1. Who was at the party?
2. What made the Jewish leaders so angry?

Question for 3s and 4s

Levi made a great big yummy dinner for Jesus. What do you think they ate?

Question for 5-7s

Levi and the other tax collectors knew that everyone else thought they were bad people, always doing the wrong thing. Who do you think Levi normally invited to his parties?

Question for over-7s

Normally, only tax collectors and sinners went to parties like Levi's. No one like Jesus had ever come to one. Who would you invite to your party who would be amazed to be invited? How would you feel about inviting them? (*It is easy to think of someone who you wouldn't normally invite. The challenge is to think of someone who would love to be invited to your party. Perhaps you would feel pleased to amaze someone, or a little cross that they get to enjoy your party without deserving it.*)

Question for teens

What do you know about tax collectors in Jesus' day? Look at the note on page 13. If you knew all this about Levi, what might you have been thinking as Levi walked with Jesus, taking him back to his house? What do you think you might have blurted out to Jesus as he walked past you? *(Some of us would want to tell Jesus all about Levi, in case he hadn't realized. Others of us might feel a little jealous that Jesus hadn't chosen to spend time with us. The best of us might want to say, "Finally! We have someone in authority who is kind to all and listens to the marginalised!")*

Think and pray

Thank Jesus that he is a friend to the friendless and to those that most people hate. Is there anyone like that who you want to pray for?

Got time to chat?

It can be lonely to feel as if you're on the outside, with people pointing at you. Sometimes we can be the ones doing the pointing. What do others do, that makes you think, "They are wrong. That is bad. They should be punished"? Sometimes we are the ones being pointed at, because we have done something wrong. Which of those two—pointing at others or being pointed at—do you think is normally you? Does this story teach you something?

Something more for the adults?

Paul was very clear that he was one of those sinners that Jesus had chosen to love. In fact, Paul said he was the worst of sinners! Read 1 Timothy 1 v 15-17. When you find yourself feeling crushed by your sin, how does Paul offer a way forward for your broken heart? Read carefully. Paul sees that he was shown mercy and patience. Jesus Christ not only offers us a way out of our shame and despair but lifts our faces to the one who offers our hearts soaring, joyful, hope-filled worship. What a Saviour we have!

DAY 3
Who is sick?

Where are we going today?

Jesus is the Doctor for those who go to him to have their sin healed.

READY?

- Open your Bible to **Luke 5 v 31-32** (or read the passage from page 18).

LET'S GO!

Pray: Dear Father, you know exactly what we are really like, and you love us so much. Please help us to understand more of what you know about us. Amen.

Perhaps try...

- **Do it, if you can!** Imagine that your floor, from left to right, has a scale from 1 and 10. Use it to score yourselves on the following questions: How slow or fast are you at running? How hungry or full are you? How tired or awake are you? How mean or kind are you?

- For each question, each of you can stand in the place for your score between 1 to 10. For younger children, don't talk about the numbers. Explain that a super-hungry person would stand by this wall, and so on.

- Imagine we have a world champion sprinter in the room and we score ourselves on how fast we are compared to them! Or imagine we have Jesus in the room. Would that change the scores you give yourself?

- If you can't do this activity, ask a quick question instead: On a scale of 1 to 10, how fast do you think you are? How hungry do you feel? How kind are you?

- *Link: In today's story, Jesus asks how sick with sin his listeners are. How would they score themselves?*

This week's story

- *Where are we in the Bible?* Levi left everything to follow Jesus. He celebrated with a party for Jesus and all of the worst people he knew. Then the people who thought they were good complained. How will Jesus explain this?

- *Look out for* Jesus explaining who he had come for.

- *Read* the passage.

Luke 5 v 31-32

[31] Jesus answered them, *"Healthy people don't need a doctor. It is the sick who need a doctor.* [32] *I have not come to invite good people. I have come to invite sinners to change their hearts and lives!"*

Questions for us all

1. At Levi's party, who were like the sick people who knew they needed a doctor? Who was the doctor?

2. How would the tax collectors have scored themselves, 1 to 10, on the sinner scale? And what about the Pharisees and religious teachers?

Question for 3s and 4s

Who did Jesus say should go to a doctor?

Question for 5-7s

Who did Jesus say he came to help?

Question for over-7s

How would Jesus score himself on the 1 to 10 scale: as a sinner or as perfect? Let's say his answer is right (because Jesus always is!). So what would the score be for the tax collectors, for the religious leaders, and for YOU? (*Let's be clear, Jesus is on 10 all day long! Tax collectors? Let's say 1. Religious leaders? Maybe 3? You and me? Tricky. But Jesus is amazing. That's why we need Jesus.*)

Question for teens

Reading Jesus' words, we're left thinking that he's saying, *If you're well, you don't need a doctor. If you're good, you don't need me.* Most of the time, most of us feel well and pretty good. So why do we need Jesus? *(We're often well enough to not need a doctor, but we're never good enough to not need Jesus! We'll see that if ask two questions. Firstly, how good is Jesus? Secondly, we're made to live for God, as Jesus did, so how are we doing at that?)*

Think and pray

We know that Jesus stands at 10/10 on the sinner/perfect scale. So what do you want to say to him? Have you got a sorry prayer? Have you got a thank-you prayer? (And if you have a please prayer, then you have the full set!)

Got time to chat?

These two verses make us feel as if the doctor is diagnosing our hearts. Do they make your heart sink as you feel the disease of sin, a disease that makes you want to smash down the doctor's door to find his healing hands? Do they make your heart proud, like the religious leaders, as you look down on others who are so much worse than you? Or do you hear these verses and your heart is so thankful, bursting with joy because you hear the doctor saying, *Go home, I have healed you. Your sins are forgiven. You are ready to meet God as "Righteous".* How will your heart feel today?

Something more for the adults?

Perhaps now we are older, no longer children, we don't need convincing that we are sick and in need of a doctor. Read Psalm 41. This was written by King David when his heart felt sick, when everyone else stood around him pointing at his sick heart. He felt low, condemned and isolated. But he knew that he should go to his doctor, and his heart was lifted and healed, and found the reason to praise God. "Praise be to the LORD, the God of Israel, from everlasting to everlasting. Amen and Amen" (Psalm 41 v 13, NIV).

Hit the Heart

DAY 4
Healed and forgiven

Where are we going today?

Jesus came to heal us by forgiving us. What a relief!

READY?

- Open your Bible to **Luke 5 v 31-32** (or read the passage from page 21).

LET'S GO!

Pray: Dear Father, please help us to feel the joy that comes from being healed. Amen.

Perhaps try...

- **Optional.** Act out opposite emotions or situations. So if one of you pretends to be thirsty, then someone else has to pretend to drink a big glass of water. If one of you is sunbathing, someone else can be holding an umbrella. Or if one of you is climbing a tree, someone else could be digging a hole.

- If you can't do this activity, ask a quick question instead: What is the opposite of each of these? Sunny, standing, clean, tired, healthy?

- *Link: Today we see that it is only Jesus who takes us from total sickness with sin to the opposite.*

This week's story

- *Where are we in the Bible?* Jesus chose to spend time with the worst of people. The religious people could not understand it, as they tried to stay well away from the tax collectors, who were known for stealing and cheating.

- *Look out for* who Jesus said he was like.

- *Read* the passage.

Luke 5 v 31-32

³¹ *Jesus answered them, "Healthy people don't need a doctor. It is the sick who need a doctor. ³² I have not come to invite good people. I have come to invite sinners to change their hearts and lives!"*

Questions for us all

1. Jesus is like a doctor. What does a good doctor do?

2. Who did Jesus go to so that he could heal them in this week's story?

Question for 3s and 4s

Would you rather be sick or well? How does it feel when you are sick?

Question for 5-7s

Why did Jesus say that he was like a doctor? Do you think he has healed your heart?

Question for over-7s

How do you think it would feel to be healed from a serious illness? Jesus says he is like a doctor. How does this help you to understand the difference he makes to us?

Question for teens

Most of us do not spend our time skipping down the street singing because of how amazing it feels to be forgiven by Jesus. If that's true of you, next time you feel flat, or find yourself questioning the value of being a Christian, what would you like to remember from this week's story? *(Can you imagine the relief of walking out of a doctor's surgery after being told that your cancer was gone? Say out loud what your first words would be in this situation. Now slightly change those same words, with that same sense of relief and joy, to sum up the change Jesus makes to your life when he forgives your sin.)*

Think and pray

Just pray prayers of thanks! Let them tumble out. Short prayers, one after another. If you run out of things to say, think about what you would say to a doctor who made you better. Can you say those same words to Jesus?

Got time to chat?

The word "gospel" means "good news". The Bible uses this to describe Jesus' rescue. This week, we have seen that good news. The calling of Levi becomes a party. Following Jesus means joy, and it leads to a party. How sad that the religious leaders were bitter, grumpy and angry. The good news of Jesus Christ is the best solution to bitterness, grumpiness and anger. How are we going to keep the party going?

Something more for the adults?

Jesus says the obvious: the sick need a doctor. Sickness starts off by being uncomfortable, inconvenient and tiring. If the sickness remains, it becomes unsettling, reducing our confidence and limiting our choices. Eventually, we would all go to the doctor, some faster than others. We would easily be able to answer the doctor's question, "How can I help?" If we were sick and didn't go to the doctor, it would become more and more baffling to those who love us. We don't have to ponder physical sickness long before we understand the power of Jesus' metaphor. Have we understand our need of Jesus? Have we understood our dependence on him? Or is he a lifestyle choice or a habit or just a good friend? Take time to talk to your Doctor. Answer his question: *How can I help?*

DAY 5

Does Jesus know?

Where are we going today?

Jesus was kind to the woman that no one else would go near.

READY?

- Open your Bible to **Luke 7 v 36-39** (or read the passage from page 24).

LET'S GO!

Pray: Dear Father, please give us soft hearts to love the people that no one else loves. Amen.

Perhaps try...

- Take off your socks and shoes.
- Are you willing to touch each other's feet? What about pushing your fingers between their toes?
- If you can't do this activity, ask a quick question instead: How would you feel about washing each other's feet?
- *Link: It is embarrassing to wash someone else's feet. In Jesus' day, only the least important people would wash another person's feet. Look who washes Jesus' feet...*

This week's story

- *Where are we in the Bible?* Jesus was getting noticed by everyone because of his teaching and miracles. Now the religious leaders were trying to work out whether Jesus was on their side or not—so they invited him to dinner to get some answers.

- *Look out for* the clues that this woman is not a welcome guest at the meal.

- *Read* the passage.

Luke 7 v 36-39

³⁶ *One of the Pharisees asked Jesus to eat with him. Jesus went into the Pharisee's house and sat at the table.* ³⁷ *A sinful woman in the town learned that Jesus was eating at the Pharisee's house. So she brought an alabaster jar of perfume.* ³⁸ *She stood at Jesus' feet, crying, and began to wash his feet with her tears. She dried his feet with her hair, kissed them many times and rubbed them with the perfume.* ³⁹ *The Pharisee who asked Jesus to come to his house saw this. He thought to himself, "If Jesus were a prophet, he would know that the woman who is touching him is a sinner!"*

Questions for us all

1. What do you think Jesus' feet would have been like after a long walk to the Pharisee's house? (Think about wearing sandals on dirt roads that are used by animals.)

2. What clues can you find that show how the Pharisee felt about this woman?

Question for 3s and 4s

What did the woman do for Jesus?

Question for 5-7s

The woman didn't just wash the muck off Jesus' feet with a sponge. Explain all the things she did.

Question for over-7s

Simon, whose house it was, said that if Jesus knew who this woman was and what she had done, Jesus would never have let her touch him. So why did Jesus let her touch him? *(We know that Jesus always knows EVERYTHING about EVERYONE. He wanted this woman to know that he loved her when no one else did.)*

Question for teens

In that culture, a woman would only let her husband see her with her hair down. It was something secret, intimate and special for someone to see a woman with her hair down. Can you think of any reason why this woman would have let her hair down for Jesus? What do you think she knew of Jesus that caused her to act like this?

Think and pray

What is wonderful about Jesus in this story? Thank him for being like this. Pray for anyone you know that everyone else pushes away or just ignores.

Got time to chat?

Children and young people can be excluded from friendship groups without a second thought. Hurtful words are thrown around too easily. Perhaps you know what it is like either to push others away or to be pushed away? What does Jesus have to say, from this story, to those who push others away as well as to those who feel that loneliness and rejection?

Something more for the adults?

Normally our shame and guilt is private. Occasionally those poor decisions, terrible mistakes and shameful actions are "out there" and known to others. Whatever her case, this woman modelled how all of it can be taken to Jesus. He is the one who already knows every single dark corner in our lives. There is a great relief, and even joy, in coming to Christ, even as we weep over our sin, knowing that he will allow us to stay. As we lay out our sin, he will never be shocked, he will never be appalled, and he will never despair.

Be ready for tomorrow!

Collect a few items that your family members could imagine being desperate to buy if they saw them in a shop. These could be yummy foods, sweets or favourite toys.

DAY 6
Who loves more?

Where are we going today?

If you are forgiven by Jesus, you will love him.

READY?

- **Do it if you can!** Collect a few items that your family members could imagine wanting to buy if they saw them in a shop. These could be yummy foods, sweets or chocolates, or favourite toys.

- Open your Bible to **Luke 7 v 40-43** (or read the passage from page 27).

LET'S GO!

Pray: Dear Father, let us see what you have done for us so that we can love you even more. Amen.

Perhaps try...

- Place some of the items you have collected in front of each family member. They can't be touched. One family member needs a bigger pile of items than the others. Put ten items in front of one person but one or two in front of the others.

- Ask your family to imagine that they have each walked into a shop and chosen these items to buy. They go to pay but find that they only have one small coin each to pay with. That's not enough! How would they feel?

- Now imagine the person at the checkout says, "Don't worry. I'll pay for you. Keep your coin. You can take your shopping."

- Now how would you feel? What would you say?

- Look at someone else's pile. Do you think they would feel differently to you? Do you think they would say anything different to you?

- If you can't do this activity, ask a quick question instead: Imagine that you're in a restaurant. It's the end of the meal. The waiter gives everyone a free chocolate but he gives you a huge free ice-cream sundae. How would you all feel about him?

- *Link: In today's story, Jesus tells a story just like this to help us understand why some people love Jesus more than others.*

This week's story

- *Where are we in the Bible?* Jesus was having dinner with some super-important people when an uninvited woman walked in and started washing Jesus' feet. She used her tears and her hair. And there's more! Everyone in the room knew her because of her bad decisions and her embarrassing mistakes. It was Simon, whose house it was, who spoke up first. He was shocked that Jesus would let the woman touch him.

- *Look out for* whether you think Simon gets the answer right.

- *Read* the passage.

Luke 7 v 40-43

⁴⁰ *Jesus said to the Pharisee, "Simon, I have something to say to you."*

Simon said, "Teacher, tell me."

⁴¹ *Jesus said, "There were two men. Both men owed money to the same banker. One man owed the banker 500 silver coins. The other man owed the banker 50 silver coins.* ⁴² *The men had no money; so they could not pay what they owed. But the banker told the men that they did not have to pay him. Which one of the two men will love the banker more?"*

⁴³ *Simon, the Pharisee, answered, "I think it would be the one who owed him the most money."*

Jesus said to Simon, "You are right."

Questions for us all

1. Imagine these two men. They have to give money to the bank. How much do they each have to give? (*If you still have the items from "Perhaps try...", put two piles in front of your family—one much bigger than the other. Point to these piles for these questions to help your family to understand.*)

2. What did the banker decide to do when he realised that the men had no money to pay?

Question for 3s and 4s

If I offered you one chocolate button or ten, which would you choose?

Question for 5-7s

Jesus asked Simon, "Which of these two men would love the banker more—the man who had to give 50 coins or the man who had to give 500 coins?" If Jesus had asked *you* that question, what would you have said?

Question for over-7s

Can you work out why Jesus told Simon this story? *(Jesus told this story to show why the Pharisee and the woman were different. Which man in the story is the woman like? Which man is Simon like? Now we start to see why she wanted to wash Jesus' feet.)*

Question for teens

In verse 39, Simon thinks, "If Jesus really is who he says he is, then he would know who this woman is and he wouldn't let her touch him." So why didn't Jesus send the woman away? Why doesn't Jesus send us away? *(Jesus wanted the woman to have the chance to love him. Jesus wants us to have the chance to love him. He wants our love.)*

Think and pray

If you have been forgiven, how much do you love Jesus? Thank him for his forgiveness. Thank him for the love you feel for him.

Got time to chat?

The bigger the sin, the bigger the shame, the bigger the guilt, the bigger the forgiveness, the bigger the love.

Is it really that simple? Whatever we did can be forgiven? I can imagine some really terrible things—really awful, horrible things. Now imagine how you'd feel after doing them—how heavy it would feel, how knotted up your heart would be.

Now imagine Jesus just taking it away, rubbing it out, lifting the weight off you, untangling your heart. How would you feel about Jesus, if you knew you were free, forgiven, washed clean? Do you believe Jesus can do that? Do you believe you could love him as much as this woman?

Something more for the adults?

Jesus gave his host, Simon, a lesson in accountancy, with numbers and calculations. Perhaps that was how Simon's heart worked. He understood money and debt. Would his heart overflow with love for Jesus as a result?

King David had a different approach. Read Psalm 103 v 1-5. David is also considering how much he loves the one who has forgiven all of his sin. His way is with words, not numbers—with poetry, not accountancy. Whichever way you prefer, let your love for God grow as you feel the freedom of living without your past sin. Read these words as a prayer and feel David's joy as your own.

DAY 7

You are saved!

Where are we going today?

Jesus was clear: the woman left saved, forgiven and friends with God.

READY?

- Open your Bible to **Luke 7 v 44-50** (or read the passage from page 31).

LET'S GO!

Pray: Dear Father, sorry that we quickly think we are better than others. Please help us to learn from Simon's mistake. Amen.

Perhaps try...

- **Do it, if you can!** Today's story is a conversation, so doing an activity might help to make the big idea of the conversation more tangible.

- Play a game called "What's just happened?" For a few of these scenarios can your family act out or talk about what you would do immediately afterwards? Perhaps one of your family could step out of the room, and then come in to see you acting it out. Can they guess what has just happened?

  - You have just arrived back from a great holiday. Or you have just got out of bed. Or you have just won the World Cup. Or you have just finished a huge meal.
  - Finish with... You have just been rescued by the pool lifeguard when you were in real danger.

- Or just ask a quick question: If you had just been rescued from drowning by a pool lifeguard, what would be the next five things you would say or do?

- *Link: We act differently because of what has just happened. In today's story, Jesus explains that the woman acted differently because of what had happened to her.*

This week's story

- *Where are we in the Bible?* Jesus was at a posh dinner when a woman barged into the fancy meal. Probably everyone else was embarrassed by this crying, shameful woman who was washing Jesus' feet with her tears. She loved so much because she'd been forgiven heaps.

- *Look out for* what Jesus said about her as she left the party.

- *Read* the passage.

Luke 7 v 44-50

⁴⁴ *Then Jesus turned toward the woman and said to Simon, "Do you see this woman? When I came into your house, you gave me no water for my feet. But she washed my feet with her tears and dried my feet with her hair.* ⁴⁵ *You did not kiss me, but she has been kissing my feet since I came in!* ⁴⁶ *You did not rub my head with oil, but she rubbed my feet with perfume.* ⁴⁷ *I tell you that her many sins are forgiven. This is clear because she showed great love. But the person who has only a little to be forgiven will feel only a little love."*

⁴⁸ *Then Jesus said to her, "Your sins are forgiven."*

⁴⁹ *The people sitting at the table began to think to themselves, "Who is this man? How can he forgive sins?"*

⁵⁰ *Jesus said to the woman, "Because you believed, you are saved from your sins. Go in peace."*

Questions for us all

1. Jesus had a long list of what Simon did *not* do? Awkward! What is on Jesus' list?

2. What did the woman do that Simon didn't?

Question for 3s and 4s

Jesus told Simon all the kind things the woman had done. Are you ready to copy what the woman did as I read out the list? "She washed Jesus' feet with her tears and dried his feet with her hair... She kissed Jesus' feet from the moment he arrived... She rubbed his feet with perfume." Can your child show what it looked like to wash feet, kiss feet and rub perfume into feet?

Question for 5-7s

You can tell that the woman had been forgiven because she loved Jesus so much. Can you tell if Simon loved Jesus? How can you tell?

Question for over-7s

The woman arrived, and all the important men would have been embarrassed. They knew what she was like and what she had done, and they thought only ugly thoughts about her. How do you think she felt as she left? *(She didn't care what anyone else thought of her. Jesus loved her, and that was enough for her.)*

Question for teens

How are you tempted to decide on someone's value? What makes you think, "They're worth knowing" or "I want nothing to do with them"? We often make these decisions in a split second. Think about what goes through your mind in those split seconds. God's love for sinners is based on his grace and not on our value. So how does Jesus think about people? *(Firstly, every created person is precious to Jesus. Secondly, we see in the Gospels that Jesus took special care of those who were ignored, hated, despised and marginalised, as in this story.)*

Think and pray

Imagine that the woman waited outside to see Jesus after his meal. What do you think she would have said to Jesus? I'm sure she would have said, "Thank you!" But what else? What would *you* like to say to Jesus?

Got time to chat?

In this story we see how the woman was changed by being forgiven; that changed how she felt, the way she behaved, and the decisions she made. It even made her brave enough to walk into a stranger's house! Why would Jesus' forgiveness make us brave? Why would Jesus saving us make us love him? Why would Jesus' love for us mean that we love others that no one else loves?

Something more for the adults?

Yesterday we looked at the first part of Psalm 103. Read Psalm 103 v 6-12. David's understanding of God gives us insight into Jesus' decisions. He expresses the same incredible joy that the woman showed in her love for Jesus. It's almost as if this psalm is the explanation of today's story. If you've read these verses, I'm sure you'll want to read all the way to the end! Drink it in. And of course, finish where David finishes, in verses 19-22, with loud, joyful praise and worship for the Lord. That's always a good place to end our prayers and songs!

DAY 8
Thankful

Where are we going today?

When Jesus forgives us, we are thankful.

READY?

- **Optional.** Gather together five objects that could represent gifts of different values, such as an apple, some money, a piece of jewellery, a computer and a car key.

- Open your Bible to **Luke 7 v 37-38 and 47-48** (or read the passage from page 34).

LET'S GO!

Pray: Dear Father, thank you that our lives can be full of thankfulness. Help us to see how. Amen.

Perhaps try...

- Imagine giving each of the gifts to one another.

- Act out the different levels of thankfulness for each one. For the cheapest gifts perhaps you would look disappointed, but for the most expensive you would go wild!

- If you can't do this activity, ask a quick question instead: Can you remember receiving a disappointing gift?

- *Link: In real life, you would be so thankful for the biggest gift. Today we see how thankful we would be for the biggest gift possible.*

This week's story

- *Where are we in the Bible?* Want to try some quickfire questions? Five seconds per answer. No pauses. Only one sentence each. Adults join in.

  - Who was hosting the dinner?
  - What sort of people were there?
  - Who burst in uninvited?
  - What did she do for Jesus?
  - How did the Simon feel about this?
  - Who loved Jesus more, the woman or Simon the religious leader? Why?

- *Look out for* how the woman shows her thankfulness.

- *Read* the passage.

Luke 7 v 37-38 and 47-48

37 A sinful woman in the town learned that Jesus was eating at the Pharisee's house. So she brought an alabaster jar of perfume. 38 She stood at Jesus' feet, crying, and began to wash his feet with her tears. She dried his feet with her hair, kissed them many times and rubbed them with the perfume.

47 [Jesus said to Simon,] "I tell you that her many sins are forgiven. This is clear because she showed great love. But the person who has only a little to be forgiven will feel only a little love."

48 Then Jesus said to her, "Your sins are forgiven."

Questions for us all

1. Why did the woman wash Jesus' feet, even though it was messy and embarrassing?

2. Why didn't Simon do anything for Jesus?

Question for 3s and 4s

How do you thank people? Is there something you say? Sometimes do you give them a hug? How would you thank Jesus?

Question for 5-7s

What would you do to thank someone for something HUGE? And then, tomorrow, would you thank them again? That's how we feel about Jesus when we understand how he has forgiven us! We want to just keep thanking him for how he has loved us.

Question for over-7s

Can you think of one way in which you have needed to be brave being a Christian? Would it feel different if you were bursting with thankfulness for Jesus' forgiveness?

Question for teens

When do you remember feeling so thankful? What would it take for you to collapse to your knees and cry tears of thankfulness, in a show of embarrassing gratitude? Could that ever be you? Would you want it to ever be you?

Think and pray

When we feel low, cross or sad, it's great for our hearts to thank God for five (or ten!) things. Fire out some thank-you prayers. Just answer the question "What makes me smile?" Thank God for every answer to that question. What a great feeling! Smiling yet?

Got time to chat?

There will always be more that we want. If someone always felt like that—wanting more, complaining—what would we expect them to be like? If that person sat next to us in class, what would they be like?

Now think about the woman in the story. She was excluded by most people, with them whispering about her and pointing at her—but she was so thankful to Jesus. His love was enough for her. She left full of peace. If someone like her sat next to us in class, what would we expect them to be like?

Something more for the adults?

Read Colossians 3 v 15-17. Read one sentence at a time. Read it again. Ask yourself the question "How does that help me to feel thankful?" Meditate on these words. Imagine the person who lived these words. Wouldn't you want them as a friend? This person would be at peace, constantly thankful, often singing, usually mumbling prayers of thanks under their breath throughout the day, living an adventurous life for Christ, free of others' expectations, living for an audience of one. Ready to give thanks?

DAY 9

A proper welcome for a crowd

Where are we going today?

Jesus loved the crowd by telling them about his kingdom and healing their illnesses.

READY?

- **Optional.** Can you find a large sheet of paper and some felt-tip pens?
- Open your Bible to **Luke 9 v 10-11** (or read the passage from page 37).

LET'S GO!

Pray: Dear Father, help us to see how Jesus loved, so that we can love in the same way. Amen.

Perhaps try...

- Who would you be most excited to have visit your home?
- What would you do to your home so that when they arrive they can see that you love them?
- Draw on the paper what you would do to welcome them.
- If you can't do this activity, ask a quick question instead: How do you welcome people you love into your home?
- *Link: Today we're going to see that Jesus welcomes people differently to the way we would.*

This week's story

- *Where are we in the Bible?* Jesus' disciples/apostles had just come back from a long trip. Jesus had sent them off without him to tell people about him and to heal them. So now that they're back, Jesus wants to take them somewhere quiet and find out how it went.

- *Look out for* what happens that stops the place being quiet.

- *Read* the passage.

Luke 9 v 10-11

¹⁰ When the apostles returned, they told Jesus all the things they had done on their trip. Then Jesus took them away to a town called Bethsaida. There, Jesus and his apostles could be alone together. ¹¹ But the people learned where Jesus went and followed him. Jesus welcomed them and talked with them about God's kingdom. He healed those who needed to be healed.

Questions for us all

1. Did you hear why Jesus had taken his friends to that place?

2. Why do you think the crowd of people followed Jesus?

Question for 3s and 4s

Did you hear who followed Jesus and the disciples?

Question for 5-7s

Jesus saw the crowd following him. He wanted to give them the best possible welcome, to make them feel so loved. What did he do?

Question for over-7s

If Jesus wanted to give the crowd the best possible welcome, why do you think he chose to heal them and to explain his kingdom? Of all the things he could have done and talked about, why do you think he chose those? *(Jesus knew that everyone needed to know about his kingdom. It's still true today. More than maths, good manners or how to ride a bike, everyone needs to know about Jesus and his kingdom.)*

Question for teens

Imagine you have unlimited money and can give your friends anything. What would you love to give them that would make you excited too? What would you choose? Now compare those gifts with the good news of the kingdom of God, which Jesus taught to the crowd that day. How would you feel about giving that to your friends? Explain what you're thinking.

Think and pray

Thank Jesus for those people who told you about him. Thank him for those people in your life who keep giving you what you need the most.

Got time to chat?

If you want your friends to hear more about Jesus, can you think of five people, and some places or ways in which they can hear more? Have each of you got two people you pray for regularly, asking that they might hear more about Jesus Christ?

Something more for the adults?

Read Psalm 119 v 97-104. Every word from God is good. Every command he gives is rooted in his love for us. Take particular notice of verse 103. This is why Jesus took the time to teach—because God's words, to those with ears and hearts to hear, are like the sweetest honey. Delicious! Good enough to savour slowly. Nourishing to the soul. If you have any experience of God's word being that sweet, then thank him that he has so changed your heart to appreciate and enjoy what you need more than anything else.

Be ready for tomorrow!

Find some chocolate or sweets/candies or something else that is an absolute treat.

DAY 10
Feeling hungry

Where are we going today?

The huge crowd ached with hunger, and the confused disciples couldn't feed them. Jesus was getting ready to teach them all a lesson.

READY?

- **Do it if you can!** Find some chocolate or sweets/candies or something else that is an absolute treat.

- You might also want playdoh/plasticine or pencil and paper for the 3-4s question.

- Open your Bible to **Luke 9 v 12-14** (or read the passage from page 40).

LET'S GO!

Pray: Dear Father, thank you that you have given us more than we need. Help us to see that, without you, we would have nothing good. Amen.

Perhaps try...

- Place the treat in the midst of your family. Ask them to sit in silence looking at it for ten seconds. Then ask, "What would each of you like to do now?"

- Can you feel the hunger in your stomach? Do you feel an ache for that treat?

- If you can't do this activity, ask a quick question instead: When were you last absolutely starving?

- *Link: Let's see that aching hunger in the Bible story today.*

This week's story

- *Where are we in the Bible?* The crowds had followed Jesus and his disciples as they went off to the middle of nowhere for some peace. And that was fine while Jesus was thrilling them all with stories about his kingdom. But it was getting late and the disciples' tummies were starting to rumble.

- *Look out for* all the problems that the disciples/apostles had.

- Read the passage.

Luke 9 v 12-14

 12 Late in the afternoon, the 12 apostles came to Jesus and said, "No one lives in this place. Send the people away. They need to find food and places to sleep in the towns and countryside around here."

13 But Jesus said to them, "You give them something to eat."

They said, "We have only five loaves of bread and two fish. Do you want us to go buy food for all these people?" 14 (There were about 5,000 men there.)

Jesus said to his followers, "Tell the people to sit in groups of about 50 people."

Questions for us all

1. Can you make a list of the different problems the disciples had? See if you can find three or more.

2. The disciples told Jesus to send the people away. What were they worried about? What did they think would go wrong?

Question for 3s and 4s

What food did they find? (Do you want to draw that or make that out of playdoh or plasticine?)

Question for 5-7s

When you're really hungry, who do you go to for food? What do they normally give you?

Question for over-7s

How do you think the disciples were feeling when Jesus told them to feed the whole crowd? Why do you think Jesus asked them to do something impossible? (*Jesus asked them so they would understand that they could not help the crowd on their own. They needed Jesus to do it for them.*)

Question for teens

The crowds were clear: *We're hungry. We need food.* The disciples were clear: *We don't have enough food to feed them. We need help.* When did you last realise that you can't go it alone, that you can't fix everything, and that you don't have what it takes?

Think and pray

Jesus used the crowd's hunger to show that the disciples and the crowd needed him. Tell Jesus what you need. Tell Jesus how you need his help.

Got time to chat?

Usually our children have everything they need. If they have a home, some food, a loving family, a school, a doctor and some friends, then it can seem to them that they don't need God. Or perhaps, parents can feel like the God of their children, always fixing every problem, always providing for their every need.

When there is a problem in our families, it can be an opportunity to learn that our heavenly Father God is always our provider. We do need him, he is in charge and we do depend on him. That creates a precious time to chat.

Something more for the adults?

Read Psalm 121 v 1-2. Are you in a time of need? Can you identify with this experience of looking to the horizon for help, desperately hoping that from far off will come your Saviour? Have you looked up and wondered where your help will come from? Do you lie in your bed wondering how you will get through tomorrow? To feel our huge need is to start to know our very real dependence on God. Is Psalm 121 a prayer to pray for yourself or someone else?

DAY 11
Satisfied

Where are we going today?

Jesus satisfied the crowds with food because he is the one who can give all that we need.

READY?

- **Optional.** Find a few armfuls of bulky, indestructible objects. Try shoes, plastic containers, cushions and teddy bears.

- Open your Bible to **Luke 9 v 15-17** (or read the passage from page 43).

LET'S GO!

Pray: Dear Father, please help us to see Jesus' power and kindness in giving the crowd all that they needed. Amen.

Perhaps try...

- Can each of you try to hold as many of the bulky, indestructible objects as you can without dropping any?

- Before you drop anything, you have to say, "You have given me enough".

- The trick is to decide when you have enough, before it gets too much. Don't get greedy!

- If you can't do this activity, ask a quick question instead: Have you ever said, "I have enough. I don't need any more"?

- *Link: When will we say, "I have enough"?*

This week's story

- *Where are we in the Bible?* A huge crowd followed Jesus and his disciples to a quiet place. That was an adventure for everyone until it got to dinner time. The disciples realised that they had one packed lunch, no shops, no houses and no clue how this was going to work. Up steps Jesus…

- *Look out for* when Jesus stopped handing out the food.

- *Read* the passage.

Luke 9 v 15-17

¹⁴ *Jesus said to his followers, "Tell the people to sit in groups of about 50 people."*

¹⁵ *So the followers did this, and all the people sat down.* ¹⁶ *Then Jesus took the five loaves of bread and two fish. He looked up to heaven and thanked God for the food. Then Jesus divided the food and gave it to the followers to give to the people.* ¹⁷ *All the people ate and were satisfied. And there was much food left. Twelve baskets were filled with pieces of food that were not eaten.*

Questions for us all

1. What did Jesus do before giving out the food? Why?

2. How much food was left over at the end? Do you think Jesus got his sums wrong?

Question for 3s and 4s

What did Jesus give the crowd to eat?

Question for 5-7s

When did Jesus stop giving out food? When everyone had had a bit each? When he ran out?

Question for over-7s

Imagine your family was in the crowd that day. You're sitting right at the front. You see what is done, and you watch as Jesus hands the food to his disciples. What would you say to each other? What questions would you ask?

Question for teens

In this meal we see that Jesus has power and generosity. That is the best possible combo. Each is amazing, but both together is a dream. Is Jesus still powerful and generous? Are there situations that make you or your friends doubt that? *(We see it at the cross and resurrection. Sometimes we see it when we ponder the goodness Jesus shows us each day. But of course, we also see places where there seems to be such a lack of generosity to those suffering the most. It is worth thinking hard about where Jesus' power is in those places. He is there. But what is he doing?)*

Think and pray

Jesus is still powerful and kind. He is still giving us all that we need. Can you each thank Jesus for the times when he has given you enough?

Got time to chat?

"I want more" is said in most families quite often. It is said by all of us, most days, perhaps silently in our hearts. There will always be others who have more than us.

Jesus said, "Blessed are those who hunger and thirst for righteousness, for they will be filled" (Matthew 5 v 6, NIV).

He also said, "But seek first [God's] kingdom and his righteousness, and all these things will be given to you as well" (Matthew 6 v 33, NIV).

Jesus is still giving us all we need, if we are hungry to be made more like Jesus. So next time we find ourselves saying, "I want more", there are some questions we could ask ourselves and each other to see what to say next: What has Jesus already given me? How has he already helped me? How has he already changed me? So do I still need more?

Something more for the adults?

Read Isaiah 25 v 6-9. There will be a better feast with a bigger crowd with more succulent food. One thing will be exactly the same: the person at the front handing out the banquet. You and I will be in that crowd, to watch closely, to listen to him speak, and to thank him ourselves. Then you will truly pray, "Thank you. You have given me enough."

Be ready for tomorrow!

Collect a range of items that represents what your family would usually want more of: a tub of ice cream (full or empty), some money, an electronic device/screen, a bag of frozen chips/fries.

DAY 12
Enough.
Thank you.

Where are we going today?

Jesus knows exactly what we need, and gives until we can say, "We have enough".

READY?

- **Do it if you can!** Collect a range of items that represents what your family would usually want more of: a tub of ice cream (full or empty), some money, an electronic device/screen, a bag of frozen chips/fries.

- Open your Bible to **Luke 9 v 16-17** (or read the passage from page 46).

LET'S GO!

Pray: Dear Father, teach us today to say, "Thank you. We have enough." Amen.

Perhaps try...

- When did each of you last say or think, "I want more"?

- Look at the collected items. Is there one there that makes you say, "I want more"? Or is the thing you always want more of not there?

- When was the last time you thought, "If only I had more X (fill in the gap!), I would be happy"?

  - Was it more friends? Because feeling left out is horrible.

  - Was it more intelligence? Because getting the lowest mark in the class makes us feel worthless.

  - Was it more ability to play a sport, to play a musical instrument, to sing, or to do art or some other skill? Because we would all love to be the very best at something!

- Was it more time with someone you love? You wish you could see them.

- Or just ask a quick question: When did you last say, "I want more"?

- *Link: Today we see a moment when everyone said, "I have all that I need."*

This week's story

- *Where are we in the Bible?* Imagine your family were in the crowd that day, as Jesus fed everyone. You've just arrived home, and your neighbour asks what you've been up to. What will you say?

- *Look out for* the moment when you would have said, "Thank you, I have enough."

- *Read* the passage.

Luke 9 v 16-17

[16] *Then Jesus took the five loaves of bread and two fish. He looked up to heaven and thanked God for the food. Then Jesus divided the food and gave it to the followers to give to the people.* [17] *All the people ate and were satisfied. And there was much food left. Twelve baskets were filled with pieces of food that were not eaten.*

Questions for us all

1. One of the crowd could have said that day, "I want more". How do you think the disciples would have replied?

2. What do you think the crowd learned about Jesus that day?

Question for 3s and 4s

What is your favourite food or drink? Which food makes you say, "I want more"?

Question for 5-7s

This week, did anything make you say, "I want more. It's not fair!"? Jesus still has the power to give us anything, and he loves us enough to be more generous than anyone else we've ever known. He still knows exactly what we need, better than we do, and he gives it to us.

Question for over-7s

Jesus knows that what we need most is a way to get back into God's family. He gave us what we need by dying on the cross. Being in God's family means we belong and we are loved. So when we wish we had more friends or were better at reading, it's like the difference between wishing you had a loving family and wishing you had more lemonade. Next time you wish you had more friends or love or food or time or intelligence or skills, what would be helpful to say to yourself?

Question for teens

We all sometimes do feel as if we absolutely need certain things. We're not imagining it. It's an ache. Just like the desperate hunger in this week's story. When we cry, or shout, or feel that we can't go on; it is real. When Jesus doesn't seem to be giving it to us, there are a few choices for how we think: *Is he not able to give us more? Does he not understand that we need more? Or does he want us to trust him when our need makes us ache?* What would it really help you to remember when Jesus doesn't seem to be giving you more, and it hurts?

Think and pray

"If only I had more X (fill in the gap), I would be happy." Tell your heavenly Father about that, and pray that you would trust him to give you what you need when you next feel that.

Got time to chat?

When someone we love feels that ache of "I want more!" it is probably not the right time to explain how Jesus gives us all we need. In that moment of ache, they probably need a hug, a listening ear and a large dollop of love. Afterwards, when the tears have stopped, then we can list the different ways that Jesus is giving us what we need in this situation. What has he given? Who has he placed there to help? How is he helping you to trust him?

Something more for the adults?

Jesus transformed the situation from empty, aching stomachs to satisfied, full stomachs. From an impatient, snappy crowd to a sea of lazing bodies, lying down on the grass by the lake. That is a picture of the change that Jesus brings about in the life of every Christian. Read John 6 v 33-37. Jesus is the bread that satisfies. He is the solution to our aching hearts. Say out loud, "With Jesus, I will never go hungry."

Be ready for tomorrow!

You will need a couple of handfuls of pasta shells, a large bottle of water, two cups, two big saucepans and ten small toys.

DAY 13

Don't be distracted

Where are we going today?

When Jesus visited, Martha was worried about doing other good things.

READY?

- **Do it if you can!** You need a couple of handfuls of pasta shells, a large bottle of water, two cups, two big saucepans and ten small toys. (Scatter the toys all over the floor.)

- Open your Bible to **Luke 10 v 38-42** (or read the passage from page 49).

LET'S GO!

Pray: Dear Father, there are so many things we could do, so please help us to understand what is most important. Amen.

Perhaps try...

- Set up three challenges that have to be attempted at the same time.

- *The first challenge* is to collect water. One of you will slowly pour water out of the bottle, from high up, into the first saucepan on the floor. The rest of the family have to catch the water using the cups and get it into the second saucepan on the other side of the room. Any water that falls into the first saucepan is lost. How much of the water can they save and get into the second saucepan? *Explain that this is the most important challenge.*

- *The second challenge* is to count how many pasta shells are in the pile.

- *The third challenge* is to tidy up all ten toys and put them on the table.

- You have the time it takes to pour the water out to complete the challenges.

- Ready? Steady? Go!

- How much of the water did you catch? How much was lost? That was the only challenge that mattered. The other two were distractions. They were good things to do, but they got in the way of the most important challenge.

- If you can't do this challenge, ask a quick question instead: When you're trying to do homework, what distracts you?

- *Link: In today's story we see how easy it is to be worried about doing good things instead of the most important task.*

This week's story

- *Where are we in the Bible?* Jesus and his disciples are stopping to visit Jesus' friends Mary and Martha, the sisters of Lazarus (John 11).

- *Look out for* what Martha is busy doing.

- *Read* the passage.

Luke 10 v 38-42

38 *While Jesus and his followers were travelling, Jesus went into a town. A woman named Martha let Jesus stay at her house.* 39 *Martha had a sister named Mary. Mary was sitting at Jesus' feet and listening to him teach.* 40 *Martha became angry because she had so much work to do. She went in and said, "Lord, don't you care that my sister has left me alone to do all the work? Tell her to help me!"*

41 *But the Lord answered her, "Martha, Martha, you are getting worried and upset about too many things.* 42 *Only one thing is important. Mary has chosen the right thing, and it will never be taken away from her."*

Questions for us all

1. What was Martha busy doing? (Also see the picture on page 51.)

2. How was Martha feeling? Why was that?

Question for 3s and 4s

If you had to look after a big group of friends in your home, what would you be busy doing?

Question for 5-7s

Jesus said that Mary was doing the best thing. What was she doing?

Question for over-7s

Martha was sure she was right. In your life, what good things can get in the way of precious chances to listen to God speaking in the Bible? *(To answer that, you need to work out when you get the chance to read the Bible on your own, to listen to it taught, and to talk about it with others.)*

Question for teens

We are all different. Some of us prefer to be busy and active. Others like to sit and talk. Some are quiet and do more listening. Do you think Mary and Martha just have different temperaments and personalities? What would you say to Martha to help her? *(Maybe Mary was normally quieter, or less busy, or even lazy. These things might all be true but there is still ONE thing to do which is best for EVERYONE.)*

Think and pray

Say sorry for sometimes making the same mistake as Martha. Martha found out she was wrong even when she was trying to be kind. It's normal to get it wrong sometimes, even when we think we're right! We're all learning from Jesus. That's why we need to keep listening to him.

Got time to chat?

It's always good to catch each other doing the right thing. Every time you see someone busy caring for others, as Martha was, we can thank them, congratulate them and encourage them. But when you catch someone listening to Jesus in the Bible, then they deserve a medal. They are winners. There is NOTHING better they could be doing. Let off party poppers! Throw them in the air! Sing a song!

Something more for the adults?

Read Hebrews 12 v 1-2. What solutions are offered to help us get through the distractions, sins and obstacles that get in the way of us reaching the finish of life's race? It can't be that easy, or we wouldn't feel so defeated by the challenges that confront us! Where do you long for Christ's help? Ask him for that help now.

DAY 14

Only one thing

Where are we going today?

Jesus said that Mary had made the best decision by sitting and listening to him.

READY?

- Open your Bible to **Luke 10 v 38-42** (or read the passage from page 53).

LET'S GO!

Pray: Dear Father, let's listen carefully to Jesus today. Please help. Amen.

Perhaps try...

- **Optional.** One at a time step out of the room, and then come back pretending to be an animal or a person.

- Everyone else has to act out what they would do if that animal or person really did walk into the room. Would you run away, rush towards it, hide, scream, get excited or look embarrassed?

- If you can't do this activity, ask a quick question instead: What would you do if your greatest living hero walked into the room right now?

- *Link: We're looking at the same story as last time, so we can think carefully about what we would do if Jesus walked in and sat speaking to us.*

This week's story

- *Where are we in the Bible?* Jesus and his friends have landed in Mary and Martha's house. Crisis! What do you do when Jesus pops into your home for a chat?

- *Look out for* what Mary does when Jesus starts speaking.

- *Read* the passage.

Luke 10 v 38-42

38 *While Jesus and his followers were travelling, Jesus went into a town. A woman named Martha let Jesus stay at her house.* 39 *Martha had a sister named Mary. Mary was sitting at Jesus' feet and listening to him teach.* 40 *Martha became angry because she had so much work to do. She went in and said, "Lord, don't you care that my sister has left me alone to do all the work? Tell her to help me!"*

41 *But the Lord answered her, "Martha, Martha, you are getting worried and upset about too many things.* 42 *Only one thing is important. Mary has chosen the right thing, and it will never be taken away from her."*

Questions for us all

1. Martha was so sure she was doing the right things. What was good about what Martha was doing?

2. What did Jesus say was the absolute best thing to be doing at that moment?

Question for 3s and 4s

Who did Jesus say made the best choice? Mary or Martha?

Question for 5-7s

Why is listening to Jesus so good? Why is it better to listen to him than to everyone else?

Question for over-7s

Can we think together of three reasons why listening to Jesus is always the best thing to do? What makes him different from others?

Question for teens

We'll come back to "listening to Jesus" in a moment. What other things do you definitely want to get done today? Now place those choices next to "listening to Jesus". Which wins your heart and why? *(What else becomes more important in your day? Getting homework done? Getting out with friends? Screen surfing? And which grips your heart most? Which feeds your soul? You can be honest.)*

Think and pray

As we have looked at this little story, we have had Jesus in the room with us, talking to us. We've learned from him, haven't we? Imagine that now he is just about to get up and leave. What do you want to say to him before he goes?

Got time to chat?

Every time you or your children open the Bible, the devil screams in your ears and into the ears of your children, *Don't bother! How could this possibly be helpful? You have so much you need to do. Get on with that. Don't waste your time with an old book, achieving precisely nothing.* You can be honest with your children by admitting that your struggle is as real as theirs. What will you say to each other in those moments? What will you pray?

Something more for the adults?

Read Psalm 1. This is a beautiful picture of what it looks like to find your delight in listening to the words of God. There will never be an end of good things to choose to do. But to prioritise the very best is going to require your heart to be certain of the beauty, the joy, and the outstanding value of listening to God. Read Psalm 1 v 2-3 and replace each "who", "whose", "that person" or "they" with your name. Do you like the sound of that?

Be ready for tomorrow!

You will need some basic building materials for two similar houses. You could use some lego, building blocks or even saucepans and baking trays.

DAY 15
Like two builders

Where are we going today?

Listening to Jesus will make our lives solid but only if we do what he says.

READY?

- **Do it if you can!** Gather some basic building materials for two similar houses. Some lego? Building blocks? Plastic cups? Saucepans and baking trays? Anything!

- Open your Bible to **Luke 6 v 46-49** (or read the passage from page 56).

LET'S GO!

Pray: Dear Father, we want to love listening to Jesus. Please help us. Amen.

Perhaps try...

- Build two identical or very similar "houses" out of your building materials. Build one on a solid surface like the floor or a table. Build the other on a cushion. Be careful now—don't let it fall over yet!

- If you can't do this activity, ask a quick question instead: What would make a good foundation if you were building a house?

- *Link: Today, we'll hear Jesus' story about two builders to explain why it matters so much that we not only listen to him but also do as he says.*

This week's story

- *Where are we in the Bible?* Yesterday, we looked at the story of Mary and Martha, seeing that listening to Jesus is the best thing to do. Today Jesus tells a parable showing the big difference between only listening to Jesus and also obeying Jesus.

- *Look out for* the difference between the two builders.

- *Read* the passage.

Luke 6 v 46-49

[46] *[Jesus said,] "Why do you call me, 'Lord, Lord,' but do not do what I say? [47] Everyone who comes to me and listens to my words and obeys [48] is like a man building a house. He digs deep and lays his foundation on rock. The floods come, and the water tries to wash the house away. But the flood cannot move the house, because the house was built well. [49] But the one who hears my words and does not obey is like a man who builds his house on the ground without a foundation. When the floods come, the house quickly falls down. And that house is completely destroyed."*

Questions for us all

1. What is the difference between the two builders?

2. How would you feel if you lived in each of these houses? How much would you care?

Question for 3s and 4s

What happens to each house? (Shall we see what happens when the house we built on the cushion is given a wobble?)

Question for 5-7s

What is the difference between the two ways that people listen to Jesus?

Question for over-7s

It sounds so simple: listen to Jesus; obey Jesus; your house stays up! But how do we listen to and obey Jesus on the football pitch, in front of a screen and with our friends? If you're not sure, who could you ask for help?

Question for teens

As we look around at our friends' lives, often they all look similar, just as the two houses in this parable look similar. Have you ever seen how someone who is obeying Jesus' words is able to stand strong when others are in danger? If you haven't, does that mean Jesus was wrong? *(Jesus doesn't tell us when the damage will happen. So it might happen at any day. Jesus did say that he came to give life to the full (John 10 v 10), so ignoring him must lead to a life that isn't the most it could be. We might see the damage being done in our lives or others' lives by ignoring Jesus' teaching but it might not happen until Jesus returns to judge all people.)*

Think and pray

When do you find it hardest to obey Jesus? Is it when you are with a group of friends? Is it when you are playing sport? Is it with your family? Pray about those times, for help to obey Jesus. Or thank Jesus that his words are the best.

Got time to chat?

The most tempting way to apply today's passage is to wait for our children to make a bad decision and then jump into the debris shouting, "See? That is what happens when you listen to Jesus but don't obey!" Instead, there are two better alternatives. First, search for the moment of obedience to Jesus' words, and encourage your child that this is building on the rock. Second, search for the moment of disobedience, wait until the raised voices have passed, and then in the calm ask what obedience to Jesus' words would have meant. Coach your child. Be on their side. Pray together. Congratulate them when they do better next time.

Something more for the adults?

"Why do you call me, 'Lord, Lord,' and do not do what I say?" (Luke 6 v 46, NIV). That stops us in our tracks. It's the stupidity of sin. We call Jesus, "My Lord" but choose to leave his words in our Bibles when we close them, rather than in our hearts. But don't stop there. Because then we read, "As for everyone who comes to me and hears my words and puts them into practice, I will show you what they are like" (v 47). It's lovely to know that Jesus has a category for us when we seek to serve him faithfully. He knows you. He sees your obedience. He sees you building on the rock. Good and faithful servant.

DAY 16
The best choice

Where are we going today?

Listening to Jesus is surprisingly hard to do, when so many other good choices can crowd him out.

READY?

- **Optional.** Find five common kitchen ingredients: such as a lemon, some sugar, some pasta, salt and an egg.

- Open your Bible to **Luke 10 v 41-42** (or read the passage from page 59).

LET'S GO!

Pray: Dear Father, please help me to believe that Jesus loves me more than anyone else and always wants the best for me. Amen.

Perhaps try...

- Lay the kitchen ingredients in front of your family.

- Name some dishes, puddings or recipes, and ask your child which of these ingredients will go into each one.

- If you can't do this activity, ask a quick question instead: What ingredients would you use to make a spaghetti bolognese?

- *Link: In that game you could have picked any of the ingredients, as they're all good. You can eat all of them. But there was always a BEST ingredient. Today we see that there are so many good things we can do but one is the BEST.*

This week's story

- *Where are we in the Bible?* Martha was doing her very best to do the right thing. And yet she still missed out on doing the best thing, which was listening to Jesus.

- *Look out for* how Jesus described the mistake Martha was making.

- *Read* the passage.

Luke 10 v 41-42

41 But the Lord answered her, "Martha, Martha, you are getting worried and upset about too many things. 42 Only one thing is important. Mary has chosen the right thing, and it will never be taken away from her."

Questions for us all

1. How did Jesus describe the mistake Martha was making?

2. Of course we can get upset about frightening things, evil people and making really bad decisions. None of those were Martha's problem. They're not usually our problem either. Martha's problem was getting worried and upset about *good* things. What good things worry us?

Question for 3s and 4s

Do you know how we listen to Jesus? How do we hear his words?

Question for 5-7s

We listen to lots of people. Can you think of people who tell you what to do? Can you think of people on screens or in sport or in music that you listen to? Are any of those people better than Jesus to listen to?

Question for over-7s

The lie we often believe is that listening to Jesus means living a boring life. Can you remember feeling as if Jesus just wants you to keep the rules, to miss out on fun or to be unpopular? *(Instead, listening to Jesus and obeying him makes us the best people we can be. That sounds fun and interesting— and the right friends will want us in their lives.)*

Question for teens

What does Jesus say is the one thing that really matters? How does that help you with the worries about what you look like, your body shape, the clothes you wear, the people who like you, the teams you're in or the grades you get?

(If you are a follower of Jesus, listening to Jesus means hearing him say that he sees you as perfect because of his death. He sees you as his own brother or sister, and his love is unconditional. It doesn't depend on anything you achieve (or don't achieve).)

Think and pray

Living in a broken world means that there will always seem to be good reasons not to listen to Jesus. Pray for Jesus to help. Talk to Jesus about when you find it hard to listen to him.

Got time to chat?

As we talk about the challenges of listening to Jesus, it will only ever make sense when we start to talk about real situations that each child actually has to deal with. What choices did they make? How did it feel? This meal particularly shows us how good choices can get in the way of the best choice. Help your children to understand when they can say "no" to good choices.

Something more for the adults?

Jesus said, "Martha, Martha, you are getting worried and upset about too many things." That word for "worried" is the same word Jesus uses in the parable of the sower when he says, "The seed that fell among thorns stands for those who hear, but as they go on their way they are choked by life's worries, riches and pleasures, and they do not mature." (Luke 8 v 14, NIV)

Martha's worries (from her desire to care) are the sort of worries that so distract from listening to Jesus that she could become totally unfruitful. That comes as a shock. We can be so worried about doing good things that we lose contact with Jesus completely. Instead, Jesus asks us to listen to him, and then to freely enjoy living for him without burden or anxiety. Can you think of occasions when you worry about doing good to the point where you lose contact with Christ? Or are you simply enjoying Christ without burden?

Be ready for tomorrow!

You will need a jar of pasta shapes.

For each member of your family, prepare two Bible quiz questions and two tasks that are acts of kindness.

DAY 17
Clever but not kind

Where are we going today?

The religious leaders knew their Bibles but were not kind to the disabled man. Jesus helped him.

READY?

- **Do it if you can!** Grab some pasta shells to use as currency.

- For each member of your family, prepare two Bible quiz questions and two tasks that are acts of kindness. Plan for the questions and the tasks to be within their ability. There are some suggestions below.

- Open your Bible to **Luke 14 v 1-6** (or read the passage from page 62).

LET'S GO!

Pray: Dear Father, please help us to not just *know* more about Jesus but to *be* more like him. Amen.

Perhaps try...

- Tell your family that you have two questions and two tasks for each of them. They will win pasta shells for right answers and completed tasks.

- Some children will become so devastated by getting a question wrong that they'll never get to the task, so do the tasks first to avoid big sulks!

- The tasks need to be acts of kindness, such as... Get a cup of water for your brother. Fetch your dad's coat. Wash up your mum's plate. Help your sister by finding her shoes.

- The questions need to be easy Bible questions such as... Noah's big boat was called a what? Baby Jesus was laid in what when he was born? What was the name of the huge man David beat? Give multiple-choice answers if the children need some extra help.

- For each completed act of kindness, give five pasta shells. For each correct answer, give one pasta shell. Then ask, "In that game, which mattered more—the right answers or being kind?"

- If you can't do this activity, ask a quick question instead: Which would you rather be: someone who always knows the right answers or someone who is always kind?

- *Link: In today's story, we see a group of religious leaders who thought they knew all the Bible answers, but they weren't kind.*

This week's story

- *Where are we in the Bible?* The Pharisees saw the crowds loving Jesus. But Jesus did everything differently to them. In today's story, it's the Sabbath (see info box on page 64). It was God's special day of rest, so if Jesus healed the man, he'd be breaking the religious laws of the Pharisees.

- *Look out for* the tricky trap they set for Jesus and what he does about it.

- *Read* the passage.

Luke 14 v 1-6

[1] *On a Sabbath day, Jesus went to the home of a leading Pharisee to eat with him. The people there were all watching Jesus very closely.* [2] *A man with dropsy was brought before Jesus.* [3] *Jesus said to the Pharisees and teachers of the law, "Is it right or wrong to heal on the Sabbath day?"* [4] *But they would not answer his question. So Jesus took the man, healed him, and sent him away.* [5] *Jesus said to the Pharisees and teachers of the law, "If your son or ox falls into a well on the Sabbath day, will you not pull him out quickly?"* [6] *And they could not answer him.*

Questions for us all

1. Dropsy is a painful disability where your legs swell up, making it hard to walk or to sit comfortably. It was the Sabbath. What was the trap the Pharisees set for Jesus? (See the note about the Sabbath on page 64.)

2. What do you think the Pharisees would say to answer Jesus' question in verse 5: *Would you rescue your son if he fell down a well on the Sabbath? What about your own ox?*

Question for 3s and 4s

How did Jesus help the man who was ill?

Question for 5-7s

The religious leaders probably wanted to talk and talk about the right answers and the right rules. Jesus just wanted to heal the man. Which matters more—talking about the right answers or being kind? Can you think of a time when you were kind?

Question for over-7s

The Pharisees wanted to show others that they were good enough for God by keeping rules. Can you think of a time when you have done the right thing just because someone is watching? Can you think of a kind act you could do secretly?

Question for teens

There is a danger that all of us slowly become more and more like the Pharisees—rule-keeping, publicly impressive but privately unkind and secretly selfish. Who would help you to become more like Jesus?

Think and pray

Talk to your heavenly Father and tell him about the sort of person you would like to be. He wants to help you to become more like Jesus. Tell him about the sort of ways you would like to be kind to others.

Got time to chat?

Everyone wants to be thought of as kind. It's not something that comes through great effort or star charts or constant reminders. It's no use shouting at someone, "Be kind!" They might be kind while you watch, but it won't last. Kindness comes from the heart: a heart that sees God's kindness and a heart that sees how unkind we can be. We can change, with the Spirit's help. The next time you catch yourself being unkind, make it a moment to pray a sorry prayer and ask God to help you change.

Something more for the adults?

Pride is the enemy of kindness. Pride looks at self the whole time. C. S. Lewis wrote, "As long as you are proud you cannot know God. A proud man is always looking down on things and people: and, of course, as long as you are looking down you cannot see something that is above you" (*Mere Christianity*). Pray that you would be someone who looks up, who has eyes fixed on the authentic Christ and who sees others as they really are.

A note about the Sabbath

God gave Moses the Ten Commandments as the starting point for how his rescued people were to live differently for him. The fourth commandment is this: "Remember to keep the Sabbath as a holy day. You may work and get everything done during six days each week. But the seventh day is a day of rest to honour the Lord your God." (Exodus 20 v 8-10, ICB)

This wonderful command to rest means that we leave time to be busy loving God. But in Jesus' time it had become a long, long list of religious rules. The leaders were on the lookout to stop almost everything on the Sabbath, including baking, writing and lighting a match. Instead of a day to love and remember God, it became a day to fear in case you accidentally broke the law.

We can keep resting for one Sabbath day every week, remembering that God still provides all we need, so while we are resting, he is still busy providing. The Jews had their Sabbath day on Saturday, but the first Christians moved it to Sunday because Jesus rose from the dead on that day. What a great way to remember each week that we are looked after by our risen, ruling King!

DAY 18
Aim low. Push others up.

Where are we going today?

One day, when we meet Jesus, he will care for those who get ignored and will push away those who are popular and important.

READY?

- **Optional.** Have a device handy for playing music.
- Open your Bible to **Luke 14 v 7-11** (or read the passage from page 66).

LET'S GO!

Pray: Dear Father, please help us to be excited to study the Bible, even in these sad stories. Help us to keep learning more about Jesus. Amen.

Perhaps try...

- Play a game of musical chairs, with one fewer chairs than the number of players. When the music stops, try to make sure it's not you who is left without a chair.
- Play again, but this time, one (or two) of you has the job of making sure everyone else has a chair. How does that change how it feels to play?
- If you can't do this activity, ask a quick question instead: Have you ever been desperate to sit in a particular seat at a meal?
- *Link: Today, Jesus tells the guests at the meal to stop fighting for the most important seat. Instead they're to try hard to put others in the important seats.*

This week's story

- *Where are we in the Bible?* Jesus is still at the meal with the religious leaders. He has healed the man with swollen legs, even though it was a trap to see if he would break their Sabbath rules. Now he turns to the guests and speaks…

- *Look out for* what Jesus has noticed about the guests.

- *Read* the passage.

Luke 14 v 7-11

[7] Then Jesus noticed that some of the guests were choosing the best places to sit. So Jesus told this story: [8] "When someone invites you to a wedding feast, don't take the most important seat. The host may have invited someone more important than you. [9] And if you are sitting in the most important seat, the host will come to you and say, 'Give this man your seat.' Then you will begin to move down to the last place. And you will be very embarrassed. [10] So when you are invited, go sit in a seat that is not important. Then the host will come to you and say, 'Friend, move up here to a more important place!' Then all the other guests will respect you. [11] Everyone who makes himself great will be made humble. But the person who makes himself humble will be made great."

Questions for us all

1. What did Jesus notice that the other guests were doing?

2. What did Jesus say was the problem with going for the most important seat?

Question for 3s and 4s

Can you see in the picture who is in the most important seat?

Question for 5-7s

Did you hear who gets to decide where everyone sits for a meal? Who gets to decide who is at the table for the best meal in heaven?

Question for over-7s

On the day when we stand before Jesus, how will he decide who is given true greatness for ever (look at verse 11)? Why do you think he tells us that now? *(He's telling us this so we won't be surprised. He wants us to be sure about how he will decide so that we make better choices now. He wants us to make choices that put others first, especially those who are lonely or ignored.)*

Question for teens

What do you think the guests were thinking as Jesus told them how to behave at parties? This was such a shock in their culture, and it's still a shock in our culture. How would the attitudes in your friendship group or in your school be transformed, if everyone realised that one day the ones who make themselves great will humbled and the humble will be made great? *(If we know that our value comes from what Jesus thinks of us, then we can aim for the floor and push others up because we know that we are loved by the only one with REAL importance.)*

Think and pray

This teaching feels so hard. How can I keep pushing others up without feeling as if I don't matter? This is why we pray. Ask God to help you trust Jesus, the best host. Who can you look after who is used to being ignored?

Got time to chat?

It hurts when we're the last ones picked or when we keep getting the lowest grade or when we finish last. It feels as if we are less than others. When Jesus' followers feel that, Jesus lifts us onto his shoulders and says, *Put this precious child on my throne.* But perhaps we're the one who keeps winning, who gets to pick the teams or who knows we'll get what we want. How does that feel? Jesus' words in this passage will help us. We can go content to be at the bottom, knowing that we will be able to look after the other ones down there with us.

Something more for the adults?

Read verse 11 slowly. And again. And again. Move your hands to show the movement described. Close your eyes. Can you say it back to yourself? Would you like to be made great by Jesus? Would you choose to make yourself humble? Start by thanking Jesus for who he is and what he is like and how he will one day gives places out at the banquet. Then pray for those you know who once exalted themselves but have been humbled. Finally, pray for yourself.

Be ready for tomorrow!

You will need some paper and pencils or felt-tip pens.

DAY 19

Strange invitations

Where are we going today?

Jesus tells us to invite forgotten and hurting people to parties because he has invited us to his forever party.

READY?

- **Do it if you can!** Find some paper and felt tips or pens/pencils.
- Open your Bible to **Luke 14 v 12-14** (or read the passage from page 70).

LET'S GO!

Pray: Dear Father, please help us to understand how much you love those who are lonely, forgotten and hurting. Amen.

Perhaps try...

- Each of you write down or draw two friends who you would invite to your party.
- Now write down or draw one person each who might love to be invited to your party—someone who doesn't normally get invited to parties. Who has just arrived in your class and has few friends? Can you think of elderly neighbours who would be thrilled to come? Do you know someone that people avoid?
- If you can't do this activity, ask a quick question instead: Do you know someone that others avoid and would never invite to their party?
- *Link: In today's story we find out why Jesus said we can invite those people we just thought of.*

This week's story

- *Where are we in the Bible?* Jesus is at the same meal. He has already healed the sick man who was brought in to trap him. He has noticed how the guests all went for the important seats at the table, and he has told them to head for the forgotten seats. Now he turns to the host, who decided who was sent an invitation.

- *Look out for* Jesus' upside-down thinking. Who does he say we should invite to parties?

- *Read* the passage.

Luke 14 v 12-14

^{12} Then Jesus said to the man who had invited him, "When you give a lunch or a dinner, don't invite only your friends, brothers, relatives and rich neighbours. At another time they will invite you to eat with them. Then you will have your reward. ^{13} Instead, when you give a feast, invite the poor, the crippled, the lame and the blind. ^{14} Then you will be blessed, because they cannot pay you back. They have nothing. But you will be rewarded when the good people rise from death."

Questions for us all

1. Who does Jesus say that people normally invite to their parties?

2. Who did Jesus tell us to invite? What sort of people are never invited to parties?

Question for 3s and 4s

Who do you want to invite to your next birthday party?

Question for 5-7s

Did you hear what Jesus said about why we usually invite our friends to our parties?

Question for over-7s

How would you feel about inviting someone poor or someone who is always sad or someone with a disability to your party? What does Jesus say he will do if we do this?

Question for teens

What are the problems with Jesus' instruction about who we should invite? What are the benefits of Jesus' instruction? *(Let's be honest, some of our friends don't want to be at a party with those who are the loneliest, the saddest and the most hurt. Perhaps we feel as if we're the ones ignored and uninvited. In those moments, if I'm a follower of Jesus, I need my heart to remember that one day I will rise from the dead and walk into Jesus' banquet. My first thought will be "Wow! How did I get invited to this?"*

Think and pray

Pray for those you know who are forgotten, lonely, poor or with a disability. Thank God that we are invited to the best party ever, and that when we get there, Jesus himself will thank us for how we have treated others.

Got time to chat?

Research tells us that those most likely to be bullied are those with a disability, those with a long-term illness, those with special educational needs, those who live in the most deprived areas, those who have been excluded from school and those from single-parent homes. In short, those most likely to live in fear and loneliness are the poor children, the crippled children, the lame children and the blind children. Rarely do children find it easy to be kind to people who are forgotten and hurting. Jesus understood that the reason we show kindness to our friends is that we are guaranteed that the kindness will be returned. Instead, can we help our children to make decisions based on how others will benefit?

Something more for the adults?

I will say this quietly and gently. Ready? Our children learn how to treat the least in society from *us*. They watch how we treat the homeless man. They listen to what we say to the mum of the disabled child. They notice who is invited into our home. They think about the prayers they hear us pray. But we cannot be the parent we wish to be. Or at least we can't yet be the parent we wish to be. We can't change to be that parent on our own.

Be ready for tomorrow! Please do this one if you possibly can.

You will need three objects to move up and down a scale. Do you have some clothes pegs that can be clipped onto a piece of string or the side of a curtain? Or have you got some blu-tac that you can stick onto a door frame?

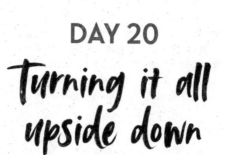

DAY 20

Turning it all upside down

Where are we going today?

Jesus warns that he will turn things upside down, putting the great at the bottom and raising the weak to the top; so think of yourself as weak.

READY?

- **Do it if you can!** You need three objects to move up and down a scale. Have you got some clothes pegs that can be clipped onto a piece of string or the side of a curtain? Or have you got some blu-tac, playdoh or sticky tape that you can stick on a door frame? The three objects will represent…

  1. "those who make themselves great"—who climb up but will one day be brought down.

  2. "those who make themselves weak"—who climb down but will one day be brought up.

  3. Jesus—who belongs at the TOP but chose to come down to bring the weak right up.

- Open your Bible to **Luke 14 v 11** (or read the passage from page 73).

LET'S GO!

Pray: Dear Father, we find it hard to choose to be weak and needy. Help us to listen and to learn how to feel weak. Amen.

Perhaps try...

- As you ask the questions, use your objects and scale to explain what Jesus meant.
- As you talk about "those who make themselves great", stick that peg/tape/object high up.
- As you talk about "those who make themselves humble", stick that peg/tape/object low down.
- As you talk about Jesus, stick his object on the ceiling!
- Then there is the big swap when your Jesus object will come down to the bottom and lift the weak up to the ceiling. And the great will be moved to the bottom.

This week's story

- *Where are we in the Bible?* Jesus has been ruining the party, telling guests that they don't understand God's law, they sit in the wrong places, and they invite the wrong people.
- *Look out for* Jesus' big swap.
- Read the passage.

Luke 14 v 11

[Jesus warned the guests,] [11] *"Everyone who makes himself great will be made humble. But the person who makes himself humble will be made great."*

Questions for us all

1. No one finds it easy to make themselves weak or humble. What sort of things would you be thinking if you were trying to make yourself weak or humble? *(Put your "weak person" object down at the bottom.) (Let us be clear that humility is not saying, "I am rubbish". Humility is saying, "I can treat that other person as more important than me".)*

2. What sort of things would you think if you were making yourself great? *(As you talk, put your "great person" object high up, but not right at the top.)* What will happen to everyone who makes themselves great? *(Put the "great person" object down at the bottom.)*

Question for 3s and 4s

Look at the picture of this story (from Day 18). Can you point to someone who feels great and rich and powerful in this story? Can you point to someone who feels weak and worth less than others?

Question for 5-7s

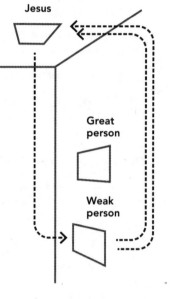

Who is the only person who can make weak people super great? Who is the only one who is actually truly great, who can turn everything upside down? (As you talk about what Jesus is really like, stick your "Jesus" object on the ceiling, far above your "great person" object. Then bring Jesus down to the "weak person" object to raise them both back to the ceiling. What a journey!)

Question for over-7s

Without Jesus in our lives, we will probably do all we can to try to make ourselves great, perhaps with many friends or with lots of trophies. Can you think of any good reasons why it is good to head for weakness at the bottom? (If we have understood how great Jesus is, we have understood the truth! We are more likely to notice others and care for them properly. If we're weak, we're also much more likely to enjoy Jesus.)

Question for teens

Some people find themselves at the bottom, without power or money or good things. Others find themselves at the top, with the chance to make choices and with great self-confidence. If you could say one thing to each group, what would it be? (Whether someone is at the bottom or the top, there is always something we can say to them about Jesus.)

Think and pray

The better we know Jesus—the more we listen to him and the more we talk to him—the more this great turning upside down makes sense. Talk to Jesus now about how you feel, what you have learned and where you are confused.

Got time to chat?

As we trust Jesus, we find out that his upside-down ways are the comfort we need when things hurt and the challenge we need when things are easy. If our child is hurt, feels alone and can't find a way to fix things, then they are more likely to be humble, with nowhere else to go for help except Jesus. If our child is carefree, enjoying opportunities and looking forward to the next success, then they are in danger of making themselves great. But Jesus is still there, asking our child to be a blessing to the weakest.

Something more for the adults?

Read Luke 13 v 22-30, just a few verses earlier, looking out for how many of today's themes are there. What is the challenge in these verses for those who are proud, strong and self-confident? What is the encouragement for those who are alienated, lonely, broken and discouraged?

DAY 21
Evil in a tree

Where are we going today?

Zacchaeus was the worst of men, but he was willing to climb a tree to see Jesus.

READY?

- **Optional.** What could you offer your family that they would do anything to get? Sweets? Extra screen time? A promise to make their favourite meal tonight/tomorrow? A promise to buy a certain special treat later?

- Open your Bible to **Luke 19 v 1-4** (or read it on page 77).

LET'S GO!

Pray: Dear Father, thank you that when we understand who Jesus is, we will do anything to see more of him. Amen.

Perhaps try...

- What treat would get you doing something bonkers? What would you do to get that favourite treat?

- What challenges could you create for each other to test how far you would go for the treat? Would you run around the block, or hold something heavy out in front of you for a long time, or stay silent for an hour, or go to bed an hour early, or do a silly dance, or wear a very surprising item of clothing? Is there a limit to what you would do?

- If you can't do this activity, ask a quick question instead: What would you be willing to do for your favourite meal?

- *Link: In today's story, we meet a man who chose to make a total fool of himself for the greatest treat.*

This week's story

- *Where are we in the Bible?* Jesus is on his journey towards Jerusalem for the final time. He has about ten days before his death. On the way, he stops in a town called Jericho.
- *Look out for* the most surprising tree-climber in history.
- *Read* the passage.

Luke 19 v 1-4

[1] *Jesus was going through the city of Jericho.* [2] *In Jericho there was a man named Zacchaeus. He was a wealthy, very important tax collector.* [3] *He wanted to see who Jesus was, but he was too short to see above the crowd.* [4] *He ran ahead to a place where he knew Jesus would come. He climbed a sycamore tree so he could see Jesus.*

Questions for us all

1. What do we know about Zacchaeus? Do you remember from Day 1 (page 13) what we know about tax collectors? Well, double that, because Zacchaeus is the *chief* tax collector. He is the only one of those that we meet in the Bible. He is the only one we would want to meet.

2. What did Zacchaeus do? What do you think others said when they saw him do that?

Question for 3s and 4s

Have you ever climbed a tree? Have you ever seen an adult climb a tree?

Question for 5-7s

Why did Zacchaeus climb a tree? How strange do you think that was?

Question for over-7s

Have you ever done something risky, difficult or embarrassing so that you or others get to see someone famous or exciting? Would you ever do that to see Jesus?

Question for teens

The normal way of things is that as we get older, we aim to have fewer embarrassing moments, behave more sensibly, and make more logical decisions. But through these meals we keep meeting people who appear to do the opposite. So what's the deal? Do Christians have to be embarrassing? What is it that we learn from these people acting so bizarrely?

Think and pray

Ask God to help you to always want to see Jesus (in the Bible!), whatever others think.

Got time to chat?

If we make decisions because of Jesus Christ, we will quickly be noticed (and often not in a good way). When we feel weak, embarrassed or ashamed because of Jesus, we might feel as if we must have done something wrong. Has this ever happened to you? What would you like to say to yourself when it happens next time? Pray for the courage to trust Jesus Christ and believe that we haven't got it wrong when we make decisions for him.

Something more for the adults?

Read Philippians 3 v 4-11. There were so many reasons why Paul might be respected. He was in many ways the opposite of Zacchaeus. Where Zacchaeus was evil, dishonest and hated, Paul was good, upright and so busy trying to do the right thing. But they both threw their pasts away, thinking nothing of being laughed at to "gain Christ". Does that sort of choice to lose everything—to not care about what others think—frighten you, excite you or confuse you?

DAY 22
With the crowd or the sinner?

Where are we going today?

Jesus chose to stay with the most hated man in the town—so the town hated him even more.

READY?

- **Optional.** Grab two types of item. You want a few items that are appealing, valuable, new and precious (e.g. money, a new toy, a box of chocolates, an unopened carton of juice). Then you want a second bunch of items that are old, worthless, tired and fit for the bin (e.g. recycling, food waste, empty food carton, dirty washing up).

- Open your Bible to **Luke 19 v 5-7** (or read the passage from page 80).

LET'S GO!

Pray: Dear Father, please show us again who Jesus came for and who we are. Amen.

Perhaps try...

- Put a pair of items before your family—one appealing item and one worthless item. Let your family pick their preference. Which would you choose?

- Separate the items into the "chosen" pile and the "rejected" pile.

- Then keep going with further pairs of items—each time separating them into either "chosen" or "rejected". By the end you will have a pile of each.

- If you can't do this activity, ask a quick question instead: Name one item you would choose that is precious and one item you would choose that is ready to be thrown away.

- *Link: In today's story, Jesus makes a choice. He chooses just one person from a huge crowd. His choice makes the whole crowd angry.*

This week's story

- *Where are we in the Bible?* Just ten days before his death, as Jesus is walking into Jericho, Zacchaeus, the most hated man in town, climbs a tree to catch a sight of Jesus.
- *Look out for* who Jesus chooses to spend some of his last hours with.
- *Read* the passage.

Luke 19 v 5-7

5 *When Jesus came to that place, he looked up and saw Zacchaeus in the tree. He said to him, "Zacchaeus, hurry and come down! I must stay at your house today."*

6 *Zacchaeus came down quickly. He was pleased to have Jesus in his house.* 7 *All the people saw this and began to complain, "Look at the kind of man Jesus stays with. Zacchaeus is a sinner!"*

Questions for us all

1. Who did Jesus choose to go home with?
2. How did the rest of the town feel about Jesus' choice?

Question for 3s and 4s

How did Zacchaeus feel about taking Jesus back to his house?

Question for 5-7s

Why were all the people so angry that Jesus had gone home with Zacchaeus?

Question for over-7s

Imagine standing in the middle of Jericho and asking the whole town, "Hands up if you think you really need Jesus to save you?" Who would put their hand up? What do you think Zacchaeus would say? Do you feel more like Zacchaeus or the crowd?

Question for teens

In 2017 a study found that 98% of British people think they're part of the nicest 50% of the population. Perhaps that day in Jericho, 98% of the town were angry that Jesus had chosen to go home with one of the 2% who knew he wasn't good. Imagine that you're standing in the crowd in Jericho. As you see Jesus choose Zacchaeus, what will you say to your friend standing next to you?

Think and pray

What we say to God now will probably depend on whether we feel more like Zacchaeus or one of the crowd.

If you feel more like Zacchaeus, you will know that you make mistakes, say the wrong things and do bad stuff. But Jesus chose Zacchaeus—and he wants to have a meal with you too. Thank him. Talk to him. Tell him how you feel.

If you feel more like one of the crowd, maybe you feel good about yourself: you try hard and usually do the right thing. Jesus sees that you try hard but wishes you knew how much you need him. Tell him how that makes you feel.

Got time to chat?

Doesn't this story show us that Jesus smashes into each day?

When our children feel broken, worthless, unable to ever get it right, Jesus says, *Let's go and have a meal together, just you and me. I can help. You are priceless to me.*

When our children are walking tall, proud, feeling they are above their friends, invincible and worthy of every award, Jesus says, *Do you think you don't need me? Just give a minute to those you're walking past, because they need me too.*

Something more for the adults?

The crowd choose *religion*: their efforts make them feel good enough, and Jesus is not needed. Zacchaeus is offered the *gospel*: his efforts will never be good enough, and Jesus is essential. Please don't be surprised if right now your heart is choosing religion. It is where every human heart goes every day. It is a miraculous work of the Spirit that every day Christ stands "under our tree" and says, "Hurry and come down! I must stay at your house today." Enjoy hosting Jesus in your home today.

DAY 23
Saved and changed

Where are we going today?

Jesus saved Zacchaeus, making him a changed man.

READY?

- **Optional.** Have you got a candle and a match? Get ready to light the candle with the match.

- Also have you got some cash; coins or notes (real or pretend) to show how much Zacchaeus is going to give away and give back. Or use some pasta shells as currency.

- Open your Bible to **Luke 19 v 8-10** (or read the passage from page 83).

LET'S GO!

Pray: Dear Father, please convince us that you will change us for the better, when we're trusting Jesus. Amen.

Perhaps try...

- Look at an unlit candle. It looks like any other object. Dead. Lifeless. You could put it in a bin right now. We wouldn't miss it.

- Now light the candle. It is totally different. You can't take your eyes off it. It behaves differently. It has changed. All because of the match.

- If you can't do this activity, ask a quick question instead: What is the greatest change you could make to yourself?

- Link: In today's story, we see that Jesus is like the match. He makes the difference to Zacchaeus, and then everything about Zacchaeus is changed.

This week's story

- Where are we in the Bible? Jesus shocked the whole of Jericho by going home with Zacchaeus, the very worst of men.
- Look out for how Zacchaeus has been changed by Jesus.
- Read the passage.

Luke 19 v 8-10

8 But Zacchaeus said to the Lord, "I will give half of my money to the poor. If I have cheated anyone, I will pay that person back four times more!"

9 Jesus said, "Salvation has come to this house today. This man truly belongs to the family of Abraham. 10 The Son of Man came to find lost people and save them."

Questions for us all

1. What did Zacchaeus say he was going to do next?
2. (Have you got that money handy?) For every £10 or $10 Zacchaeus had, how much of it would he give away? And if he had cheated anyone out of £1/$1 (and remember he had probably cheated everybody!), how much would Zacchaeus give back? (Lay money on the table to show what this giving away and paying back looks like.)

Question for 3s and 4s

Look at the picture on page 85. Which one is Zacchaeus? How can you tell?

Question for 5-7s

What was Zacchaeus like before? How is he different?

Question for over-7s

Zacchaeus is a different man. Look at how Jesus explained this change in verses 9-10. Can you find at least three ways in which Jesus has changed Zacchaeus?

Question for teens

A lot is happening here in the life of one man. He has been forgiven for an evil career, brought into God's family, cured of an addiction to wealth and transformed into the model of generosity. Which of these do you find most inspiring? Can you see any of these happening in your life, perhaps less dramatically! *(If you are trusting Jesus, I hope you can see change in your life. Sometimes others find it easier to see change happening in us. It is good to talk about that, as well as to talk about what we see and what we feel.)*

Think and pray

Most of us want to be better, kinder and more generous. Thank Jesus that he is the one who can save us and he is the one who can change us. Take time to pray for change in yourself. Then you might like to pray for someone else too.

Got time to chat?

Jesus has all power to change each of us: parents and children. He is God. Look at what he did for Zacchaeus! And yet I wonder if he can help me with my bad habit, my ugly thoughts, my wild tongue, my vicious anger or my constant sad feelings that weigh me down. Of course he can help. With Jesus' help, change is inevitable. Normally change is not as dramatic as it was in Zacchaeus, but it can be. Often though, the change is painfully slow and frustrating.

When it is calm, let's talk about the change we need. Let's be gentle with each other. Let's be confident and risk praying that dangerous bold prayer, asking Jesus to change us.

Something more for the adults?

Read 2 Corinthians 5 v 16-17. In these verses, we see what Christians really are: they have a new life with a totally new start. The old has been cut out. The new worship and love for Christ have filled the space. This is from God. Trust him. Keep listening to him. Keep talking to him.

Be ready for tomorrow!

Have ready three toy people. Maybe Lego people, action figures or things that could pass as people.

Hit the Heart

DAY 24
Lost and hated by all (except one)

Where are we going today?

Jesus forgave Zacchaeus, the worst sinner in town, because this is what Jesus came to do.

READY?

- **Do it if you can!** Do you have three toy people? Maybe Lego people, action figures or things that could pass as people? Hide them so that at least one of them will not be found. Remember where you hide them!

- Open your Bible to **Luke 19 v 5-10** (or read the passage from page 87).

LET'S GO!

Pray: Dear Father, please help us to understand that without Jesus we would all be lost. Amen.

Perhaps try...

- Can you find the hidden toy people? Go!

- How many did we find? How many are still lost?

- Shall we find the last lost people together? They're not going to be found without us.

- If you can't do this activity, ask a quick question instead: Who always finds the lost stuff in your family?

- *Link: In today's story, Jesus says that Zacchaeus was lost. Zacchaeus was lost from God—he was not in God's family and he had no way of getting into God's family on his own. He needed Jesus' help.*

This week's story

- *Where are we in the Bible?* When Jesus announced that Zacchaeus had been forgiven, saved and brought into God's family, the people would still have been confused. Why Zacchaeus of all people? Why not them?

- *Look out for* the answer to the question "Why did Jesus choose Zacchaeus?"

- *Read* the passage.

Luke 19 v 5-10

⁵ *When Jesus came to that place, he looked up and saw Zacchaeus in the tree. He said to him, "Zacchaeus, hurry and come down! I must stay at your house today."*

⁶ *Zacchaeus came down quickly. He was pleased to have Jesus in his house.* ⁷ *All the people saw this and began to complain, "Look at the kind of man Jesus stays with. Zacchaeus is a sinner!"*

⁸ *But Zacchaeus said to the Lord, "I will give half of my money to the poor. If I have cheated anyone, I will pay that person back four times more!"*

⁹ *Jesus said, "Salvation has come to this house today. This man truly belongs to the family of Abraham.* ¹⁰ *The Son of Man came to find lost people and save them."*

Questions for us all

1. Why do you think Jesus chose Zacchaeus?

2. The whole town hated Zacchaeus, and complained when Jesus chose him. Who did the crowd think Jesus should have chosen?

Question for 3s and 4s

What did Jesus do for Zacchaeus? Listen carefully as I read verse 10 again.

Question for 5-7s

Can you think of someone really naughty? Maybe they don't listen to the teacher or they hurt you or others with their words or their actions. Zacchaeus was like that—always hurting others with his words and decisions. How would Jesus want to help the naughty person you thought of?

Question for over-7s

Jesus said that he had come for the lost. If Jesus has found and saved you, then does that mean that you used to be lost? Why is Jesus good news for lost people?

Question for teens

The story of Zacchaeus helps us to understand what Jesus says to us if we feel either like Zacchaeus or the crowd. If we feel like Zacchaeus (guilty of terrible mistakes that have hurt others), what are the implications of Jesus' words? If we feel like the crowd (good, pleased with ourselves and better than others), what are the implications of Jesus' words?

Think and pray

What have you learned from this story? Do you feel so pleased to be in God's family, like Zacchaeus? Then thank Jesus that he has found and saved you. Do you feel lost, naughty and a long way from God's family? Then pray for Jesus to come to you.

Got time to chat?

As children get older, they put each other into neat categories that they usually learn from us. So children label each other as "foreign", "naughty", "fun", "Muslim", "quiet" and so on. Talk to your children about how they would describe others in their class or that they know from elsewhere. How do we think Jesus thinks about those people?

Something more for the adults?

Do you feel broken like Zacchaeus or arrogant like the crowd? Let's assume that you're feeling more broken today. Parents usually do. Read Psalm 103 v 8-18. If you're enjoying it, just keep reading! "He has taken our sins away from us as far as the east is from west" (v 12, ICB). You, too, can know Zacchaeus' joy! Your loving heavenly Father has had compassion on you. And he will again today.

DAY 25
Not the last supper

Where are we going today?

Jesus was excited about his last meal with his friends before his death, but he looked forward to a better meal together in heaven.

READY?

- Open your Bible to **Luke 22 v 7-16** (or read the passage from page 90).

LET'S GO!

Pray: Dear Father, let us feel the excitement and sadness of sitting down with Jesus for his last meal before his death. Amen.

Perhaps try...

- **Optional.** Play a game of "Eleven" (or any number your family can count up to!)

- The object of this game is to count up to eleven together. It is a team game. Your whole family wins if one of you says, "Eleven". But there are some rules, to make it a little harder than it sounds...

- Every number from one to eleven must be said out loud in order.

- No one may say two consecutive numbers. So if I say, "Five", I am not allowed to say, "Six".

- Two people may not speak at the same time. This is the hard part! There needs to be silence, and then only one person can speak at a time. If two of you make a sound at the same time, you have broken this rule. You'll find it easiest if you sit in a circle and can look at each other. (Playing this game with your eyes shut is practically impossible!)

- If any rule is broken, you go back to "One".

- If you can't do this activity, ask a quick question instead: What are you most looking forward to right now?

- *Link: Today we're hearing about Jesus' last meal with his friends before he died. But he said that there would be another meal. The next one would be the most important—and they would enjoy it together.*

This week's story

- *Where are we in the Bible?* Jesus has arrived in Jerusalem—for his death. He knows that this is his last meal with his friends. It is the Passover meal, the biggest meal in the Jewish year. (See the info box on page 92.)

- *Look out for* the word "Passover". Every time you hear it, clap once.

- *Read* the passage, clapping when you hear the special word. What is the special word we're listening for?

Luke 22 v 7-16

[7] *The Day of Unleavened Bread came. This was the day the Passover lambs had to be sacrificed.* [8] *Jesus said to Peter and John, "Go and prepare the Passover meal for us to eat."*

[9] *They asked, "Where do you want us to prepare it?"*

Jesus said to them, [10] *"Listen! After you go into the city, you will see a man carrying a jar of water. Follow him into the house that he enters.* [11] *Tell the person who owns that house, 'The Teacher asks that you please show us the room where he and his followers may eat the Passover meal.'* [12] *Then he will show you a large room upstairs. This room is ready for you. Prepare the Passover meal there."*

[13] *So Peter and John left. Everything happened as Jesus had said. So they prepared the Passover meal.*

[14] *When the time came, Jesus and the apostles were sitting at the table.* [15] *He said to them, "I wanted very much to eat this Passover meal with you before I die.* [16] *I will never eat another Passover meal until it is given its true meaning in the kingdom of God."*

Questions for us all

1. Jesus told Peter and John to follow a man with a water jug to find a room to eat in. Listen to what happened and tell me if Jesus got it right.

2. In verses 14-16, Jesus gets excited about two meals with his friends. What are those two meals? Which do you think he is most excited about?

Question for 3s and 4s

Was there lots of happy clapping? Did you hear what meal it is that Jesus and his friends are about to eat, which Luke *really* wants us to notice?

Question for 5-7s

The best parties have a big meal with friends. Can you think of three reasons why you get excited about a big meal with friends?

Question for over-7s

It sounds very strange to hear someone getting excited about a meal before their death. What is there about this meal for Jesus to look forward to so much? *(Jesus loves his friends. He wants to be with them. He wants to celebrate his death. Weird? Not at all, because it is a saving death.)*

Question for teens

Jesus said that the next time he eats this kind of meal, it will be in heaven when it will be "given its true meaning" (v 16). Imagine sitting in the new creation, at that better meal, next to Peter and John, with Jesus smiling at the head of the table. Imagine a little brother or sister sitting next to you whispering, "What's this meal for?" What would you say?

Think and pray

Would you rather give thanks for Jesus' love for his friends (which can include you) or talk to God about what you look forward to about the better meal in heaven?

Got time to chat?

Children relate to death in a slightly different way to us. Children do not sustain that level of emotion for long. So there will be moments when they feel overwhelmed with sadness, but they pass quickly and return equally suddenly. We can give our children the truth to remember in those moments of overwhelming grief. We can talk about this feast in heaven. What food will be on the table? What will you drink? Who will you sit next to? Where will Jesus be? Will anyone be crying? What are you looking forward to?

Something more for the adults?

Read Isaiah 25 v 6-9. Imagine the reality that this prophecy paints so vividly. Pick out the blessings. Which one of these is most precious to you?

A note about the Passover

The Passover meal was eaten once a year by God's people to remember the first Passover. Do you eat a big lunch on Christmas day to remember the first Christmas? It's just like that.

You can read about the first Passover in Exodus 12. It would be great to read that story this week, from the Bible or a children's Bible, as we look at the last supper together. Notice these amazing matching ideas:

- The first Passover was eaten the night before God rescued his people from Egypt. Jesus' meal was eaten the night before God rescued his people from sin and death.

- Each family had to kill a perfect boy lamb. That lamb died so that they could be rescued from slavery in Egypt to be free to live in the promised land. Jesus is our perfect male lamb, who died so that we can be rescued from the slavery of sin to be free to live for Jesus.

- The lamb died in the place of the eldest son so that death would *pass over* his family. Jesus, God's firstborn Son, died in our place so that when we trust in Jesus, death can *pass over* us and we can walk into life for ever in the new creation.

Be ready for tomorrow!

You will need some bread and something to model with (playdoh, plasticine, modelling clay, pastry or tin foil).

DAY 26
A meal
to remember

Where are we going today?

Jesus used the bread and wine to explain how his body and blood would be used to save his friends.

READY?

- **Do it if you can!** Bring some bread to the table. Have you also got some playdoh, plasticine, modelling clay or pastry? Or failing that, have you got some tin foil?

- Open your Bible to **Luke 22 v 17-23** (or read the passage from page 94).

LET'S GO!

Pray: Dear Father, please help us to see how this meal helps us to understand Jesus' death. Amen.

Perhaps try...

- Make two figures out of the material you have available. If you're using tin foil, it can be torn and scrunched into shape. One of these figures is Jesus and the other one is you. Can you make it clear that one of them is you?

- Keep the bread and these two figures to one side until needed.

This week's story

- *Where are we in the Bible?* Jesus is sitting with his best friends at a table eating his last Passover meal before his death. He understands exactly what is about to happen. They don't! How is he going to help them get it?

- *Look out for* when Jesus says, "for you". What does Jesus say he will do "for you"?

- *Read* the passage.

Luke 22 v 17-23

¹⁷ *Then Jesus took a cup. He gave thanks to God for it and said, "Take this cup and give it to everyone here.* ¹⁸ *I will not drink again from the fruit of the vine until God's kingdom comes."*

¹⁹ *Then Jesus took some bread. He thanked God for it, broke it, and gave it to the apostles. Then Jesus said, "This bread is my body that I am giving for you. Do this to remember me."* ²⁰ *In the same way, after supper, Jesus took the cup and said, "This cup shows the new agreement that God makes with his people. This new agreement begins with my blood which is poured out for you."*

²¹ *Jesus said, "One of you will turn against me. His hand is by my hand on the table.* ²² *The Son of Man will do what God has planned. But how terrible it will be for that man who gives the Son of Man to be killed."*

²³ *Then the apostles asked each other, "Which one of us would do that to Jesus?"*

Questions for us all

1. What food and what drink does Jesus use to explain his death to his friends?

2. Do you remember what meat was at the centre of the Passover meal? (See the Passover info box on page 92.) Did you hear anything mentioned in today's passage that would be like the Passover lamb? (Hint: Or *who* is the lamb in this meal?)

Question for 3s and 4s

As I read verse 19, can you act it out using the bread? Did you hear what Jesus did with the bread?

Question for 5-7s

What does Jesus say the bread is like? What happened to the bread? If you have made a Jesus figure, what can you do to it, to show that it is like the bread?

Question for over-7s

Jesus said that his body was being given for you. If I said, "I'm giving my body for you," it would sound a bit strange. If you have made a figure of yourself, what can you do to it, to show what will happen to it?

Explain that:

- Jesus' body was given for you. He chose to have his body broken for you.

- He gave his body so that our bodies can be given life for ever. Did you manage to show that with your figures?

- The death *we* deserved fell on *him*. The forever life *he* deserved fell on *us*.

Question for teens

This is the Passover meal. Jesus is the Passover lamb, who was about to die, so that if we trust in him, death will pass over you and me because it has fallen on Jesus. As you see how that death fell on Jesus, what are the different emotions you feel?

Think and pray

If you had the chance to talk to Jesus, what would you say to him after this meal?

Got time to chat?

Jesus' death for us may not be a topic of conversation that comes up often, naturally, but opportunities like this Bible time mean we can talk about the most amazing weekend in human history. This is a conversation worth going out of our way for. Take the chance to ask, "Do you believe this happened for you?" and "Do you want to trust Jesus and believe that his death is enough to save you?" These are precious conversations.

Something more for the adults?

Meditate on 1 Peter 1 v 18-19. Read it slowly at least three times. Think about what these verses mean. What is the point that Peter wants us to understand? What response can you feel growing in your heart as you chew over the words?

DAY 27
True greatness

Where are we going today?

Jesus' death for others is a lesson to his friends in how they can live to serve others.

READY?

- Open your Bible to **Luke 22 v 24-27** (or read the passage from page 98).

LET'S GO!

Pray: Dear Father, we usually try to make ourselves important by telling others what to do, and by making others feeling less important. Please help us to want to be more like Jesus. Amen.

Perhaps try...

- **Do it if you can!** Sort yourselves into age order. The eldest gives all those younger than him/her an order such as "Act like you're surfing" or "Jump up and down ten times" or "Pretend you're standing in a freezer". Then the next youngest gives all those younger a different order. And so on until everyone except the youngest has given an order.

- Now the eldest steps down to be below the youngest and asks, "What can I do for you?" All the others can now give orders.

- If you can't do this activity, ask a quick question instead: When do you tell others what to do?

- Link: Today, Jesus explains that his followers can learn from him by choosing to serve.

This week's story

- *Where are we in the Bible?* It's coming to the end of Jesus' last meal with his friends. He's already helped them understand why he will die—now he wants to teach them how to live.

- *Look out for* how Jesus tells his friends to be really great.

- Read the passage.

Luke 22 v 24-27

²⁴ *Then the apostles began to argue about which one of them was the most important. ²⁵ But Jesus said to them, "The kings of the world rule over their people. Men who have authority over others are called 'very important.' ²⁶ But you must not be like that. The greatest among you should be like the youngest, and the leader should be like the servant. ²⁷ Who is more important: the one sitting at the table or the one serving him? You think the one at the table is more important. But I am like a servant among you!"*

Questions for us all

1. What were Jesus' disciples arguing about?

2. How does Jesus say kings and important people usually treat others?

Question for 3s and 4s

Can you pretend to be very important and tell me what to do?

Question for 5-7s

How is Jesus going to put others before himself?

Question for over-7s

Why do we prefer to tell others what to do? Jesus' death can change that.

Question for teens

Imagine you spend a week serving others, looking to their needs, and making them feel important. I'm guessing that no one else would complain. So if doing this would make you so popular, why isn't everyone doing it?

Think and pray

You could thank Jesus for serving you, so there's nothing left to prove. Or pray for a chance today to look to serve others rather than to give orders.

Got time to chat?

Can we look today at those moments when we catch ourselves just as we're about to take control and make others do what we want. Let's look to turn them on their head. At those moments, parents and children, let's see what we could say next to serve others rather than to make them serve us.

Something more for the adults?

Read Philippians 2 v 1-4. As we read verses 3-4, it feels as if the bar has been set very high—unachievably so. What have we seen of Jesus today that makes this possible? How can he transform our hearts?

Be ready for tomorrow!

You will need some bread and some juice (ideally purple).

DAY 28
Do this to remember me

Where are we going today?

Jesus told his friends to keep sharing this meal to remember him, so Christians keep sharing this special meal together today.

READY?

- **Do it if you can!** Find some bread and some juice. It would be great if it was a purple drink, but use what you have got.

- Open your Bible to **Luke 22 v 15-20** (or read the passage from page 101).

LET'S GO!

Pray: Dear Father, thank you for the meal that Jesus told Christians to eat. Please bless us as you have blessed Christians throughout all time. Amen.

Perhaps try...

- Sit around a table with bread and drink in the middle.

- As you read today's Bible passage, follow Jesus' prompts. Give thanks for the drink and the bread when he does. Share the bread when he does. Share the drink when he does.

- If you can't do this activity, ask a quick question instead: Have you seen Communion or the Lord's Supper happen? What did you think of it?

- *Link: Today, we will learn about the meal that Jesus told Christians to eat to remember him.*

This week's story

- *Where are we in the Bible?* During Jesus' last meal with his friends, he explained that the bread and wine showed that his body and blood would be given for them. He also told them to keep sharing this meal after he had gone, to remember him and his rescuing death for them.

- *Look out for* what Jesus told Christians to do as we read.

- *Read* the passage.

Luke 22 v 15-20

15 He said to them, "I wanted very much to eat this Passover meal with you before I die. 16 I will never eat another Passover meal until it is given its true meaning in the kingdom of God."

17 Then Jesus took a cup. He gave thanks to God for it and said, "Take this cup and give it to everyone here. 18 I will not drink again from the fruit of the vine until God's kingdom comes."

19 Then Jesus took some bread. He thanked God for it, broke it, and gave it to the apostles. Then Jesus said, "This bread is my body that I am giving for you. Do this to remember me." 20 In the same way, after supper, Jesus took the cup and said, "This cup shows the new agreement that God makes with his people. This new agreement begins with my blood which is poured out for you."

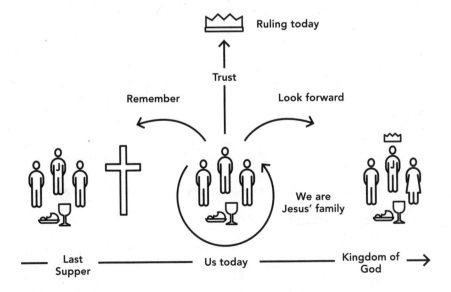

Questions for us all

1. What did Jesus want his followers to keep doing?

2. If you were helping other Christians to share this meal together, what would you tell them to do?

Question for 3s and 4s

Do you know what Christians are remembering when we share this meal?

Question for 5-7s

Jesus said that, one day, we will be with him, and we will enjoy and understand this meal even more. What are you looking forward to about that time?

Question for over-7s

Christians eat this meal to show that we still trust that Jesus' body and blood saved us. If you were finding it hard to keep trusting Jesus as your King, how would eating this meal with other Christians help you?

Question for teens

The Passover meal was always a family celebration. When Jesus changed it, to make it about himself, he shared the meal with his new, bigger Christian family. As a Christian, do you think it would help you if you regularly shared the Lord's Supper with your bigger Christian church family? (Eating the Lord's Supper together shows believers that we are one family. We can keep going together. Jesus' death has brought us into his family. Together.)

Think and pray

Thank Jesus that his meal helps his followers in so many ways.

Got time to chat?

The Lord's Supper is a meal. It is shared. It is bread and wine. It helps us to remember. But it's not like other meals. Most other meals happen because we are hungry. But the Lord's Supper happens because Jesus told his followers to share this meal together. We are obeying Jesus, and trusting that such obedience helps us.

Something more for the adults?

1 Corinthians 11 v 26 says, "For whenever you eat this bread and drink this cup, you proclaim the Lord's death until he comes" (NIV). To gather with our church family, to eat the bread and drink the cup, is much more than just sharing a meal. It is showing that Christ's death is enough for us: it is the most important event in all history; it is what defines us; it is what makes us the family of Christ.

DAY 29
Their faces were very sad

Where are we going today?

Jesus walked with his sad friends, listening to their sad story of his death. They didn't know it was Jesus—alive!

READY?

- Open your Bible to **Luke 24 v 13-24** (or read the passage from page 104).

LET'S GO!

Pray: Dear Father, you know our disappointments, our sadness and our fears. Please help us to know what to do with them. Amen.

Perhaps try...

- **Optional.** This is a long passage. To help follow the movement, surprises and great sadness, you could act it out.

- Are there three of you to be Cleopas, Bob/Sue and Jesus? Any others can watch or join the walking group. If you want an adventure, you could go outside and act it out as you walk along together.

- If you can't do this activity, ask a quick question instead: What makes you feel disappointed or sad?

- *Link: Today, Jesus met with two friends who were very disappointed with him. And they told him so!*

This week's story

- *Where are we in the Bible?* Jesus has been crucified. His body has been laid in the tomb. His friends are beyond sad. It's the Sunday afterwards and some of the women have found the tomb empty. Two other friends of Jesus are walking out of Jerusalem without hope.

- *Look out for* what has made the two friends most sad.

- *Read* the passage.

Luke 24 v 13-24

13 That same day two of Jesus' followers were going to a town named Emmaus. It is about seven miles from Jerusalem. 14 They were talking about everything that had happened. 15 While they were discussing these things, Jesus himself came near and began walking with them. 16 (They were not allowed to recognise Jesus.) 17 Then he said, "What are these things you are talking about while you walk?"

The two followers stopped. Their faces were very sad. 18 The one named Cleopas answered, "You must be the only one in Jerusalem who does not know what just happened there."

19 Jesus said to them, "What are you talking about?"

The followers said, "It is about Jesus of Nazareth. He was a prophet from God to all the people. He said and did many powerful things. 20 Our leaders and the leading priests gave him up to be judged and killed. They nailed him to a cross. 21 But we were hoping that he would free the Jews. It is now the third day since this happened. 22 And today some women among us told us some amazing things. Early this morning they went to the tomb, 23 but they did not find his body there. They came and told us that they had seen a vision of angels. The angels said that Jesus was alive! 24 So some of our group went to the tomb, too. They found it just as the women said, but they did not see Jesus."

Questions for us all

1. What has made the two friends most sad?

2. What were they hoping Jesus would do? (Take a look at verse 21.)

Question for 3s and 4s

How are the two friends feeling as they walk along? Do you know why they feel like that?

Question for 5-7s

These friends only have sadness. There is no happiness left. Is there anything that would make you feel that sad?

Question for over-7s

You know how this story ends. You know there is good news coming. But for these two friends, their world has just fallen apart. Which sadness and disappointment is fixed by Jesus' resurrection?

Question for teens

Imagine it! Jesus had died to save. He had risen from the dead to rule in glory. Yet these travellers are still disappointed with him! We know how this story ends; yet we can still feel disappointed. Do you feel disappointed with Jesus, perhaps where he hasn't fixed a problem or he has left you in doubt? Can this story help you to speak truth to yourself? *(If we trust in Jesus, we can look forward to life beyond the grave, when we will see his glory and we will sing, feeling the deepest joy. All disappointment we ever felt will be a distant memory. That certain hope can change today's disappointment.)*

Think and pray

Thank Jesus that we don't need to be disappointed and sad. He is risen! He is making all things new.

Got time to chat?

When our children feel sad, as parents we usually want to rush to fix it for them. We want to cheer them up. We would say or do anything to reduce the problem.

This week, as we look at this meal, we will learn from the expert in how to care for the brokenhearted. Jesus started by asking his friends to tell him about the problem and how they felt, even before he told them who he was. Before we offer answers, can we allow our children to explain what hurts?

Something more for the adults?

"Their faces were very sad." Is anything causing you deep sadness at the moment? Does that sadness lead you to be disappointed with Jesus? The thought can grow in our minds that, "This hurts so much. Jesus either doesn't care or can't fix it." This story offers us a prayer for when we feel that disappointment: "Dear Father, Jesus is risen, he walks with me by his Spirit, he is caring for me and he is in charge. And yet I feel disappointed. Please let me see him more clearly. Amen."

DAY 30

A stranger explains the whole Bible

Where are we going today?

Jesus showed his friends from the Bible that his death was a great victory, not an awful failure.

READY?

- **Optional.** Grab a piece of paper and a pen.
- Open your Bible to **Luke 24 v 25-29** (or read the passage from page 107).

LET'S GO!

Pray: Dear Father, please open our eyes to who Jesus is. We need your help to see more of him. Amen.

Perhaps try...

- What are the different ways of helping your family to guess a word without saying it?
- A set of words for this game might be: car, tree, cow, fridge, flower, sandwich.
  - Using the pen and paper, can one of you draw a word for everyone else to guess?
  - Can one of you act out a word (without saying anything) for everyone else to guess?
  - Can one of you describe a word using other words, without saying the name of the object, for everyone else to guess?

- *If you can't do this activity, ask a quick question instead:* When do you get so confused that you need someone else's help to understand?

- *Link: There are many ways to help others to understand something difficult, but today Jesus shows that there is one way to understand his death that is better than all other ways.*

This week's story

- *Where are we in the Bible?* Two of Jesus' friends left Jerusalem after his death, walking to Emmaus, talking about all that had happened. When a stranger (who was really Jesus) walked up to them, they explained to him that Jesus' death had left them disappointed.

- *Look out for* how Jesus helps them to understand how they had got it so wrong.

- *Read* the passage.

Luke 24 v 25-29

[25] *Then Jesus said to them, "You are foolish and slow to realise what is true. You should believe everything the prophets said.* [26] *They said that the Christ must suffer these things before he enters his glory."* [27] *Then Jesus began to explain everything that had been written about himself in the Scriptures. He started with Moses, and then he talked about what all the prophets had said about him.*

[28] *They came near the town of Emmaus, and Jesus acted as if he did not plan to stop there.* [29] *But they begged him, "Stay with us. It is late; it is almost night." So he went in to stay with them.*

Questions for us all

1. What mistake had the two friends been making?

2. How did Jesus help them to understand how his death was always part of God's plan?

Question for 3s and 4s

We don't know why these two friends didn't realise it was Jesus. Can you hide your face from your family so they don't realise it's you?

Question for 5-7s

Jesus wanted these two friends to know they were wrong to be disappointed. Did you hear what he called them (v 25)? If they had listened more carefully in Bible school (with the help of the Holy Spirit), do you know what they would have understood?

Question for over-7s

The two friends thought that Jesus' death was the biggest failure ever. Jesus put them right. Have a look at verses 26-27. Have a go at explaining what the truth is about Jesus? *(The truth about Jesus is that his death was always a key part of God's plan, clearly shown in the pages of the Old Testament. His death wasn't an awful failure—it was the great victory that had to happen before he could take up his throne in heaven.)*

Question for teens

Has anyone ever said to you, "I'd believe in God if he just made things clearer!" or "Why doesn't God just sent a thunderbolt to make me believe in him?" Jesus could have chosen so many other options: thunderbolts, angels or speaking donkeys. At the very least, Jesus could have showed them who he was a little earlier and shouted, "Ta-dah!" So why do you think he decided that explaining the Bible was the best way to help them understand why he had to die?

Think and pray

Has the Spirit helped you to understand who Jesus is? Do you know enough about Jesus to trust him? If yes, thank him, because the Spirit has done a miracle in you!

Got time to chat?

It is hard to keep trusting. It is hard to keep going. When Jesus found his friends feeling like that on the road to Emmaus, he opened the Bible with them.

When your child is feeling confused, disappointed, sad, frustrated or desperate, there will be a moment when they need the wonder of the Bible's truth to light their way. Pray for the Spirit to do that same miracle as he did for the friends at the meal table: to open your child's heart to see that Jesus is all they need to keep going.

Something more for the adults?

Don't miss the obvious point that the risen, resurrected Jesus could still enjoy a meal with friends. Jesus' resurrected body is the ready-to-test-drive model of the body we will have when we are raised from the dead. If he could slice up his food, rip the bread apart, digest the roast potatoes and wash everything down with a big gulp of his favourite drink, then we will too. If he could sit at a table with his friends, encourage them with the truth, and laugh about shared memories, then we will too.

DAY 31
Eyes opened and hearts on fire

Where are we going today?

Jesus opened the friends' eyes to see him alive in front of them, but he also set their hearts on fire to show them himself in the Bible.

READY?

- **Optional.** Find something to use as a blindfold, such as a towel. Make sure there are ten or more items on the table/floor. It doesn't matter what they are.

- Open your Bible to **Luke 24 v 30-35** (or read the passage from page 111).

LET'S GO!

Pray: Dear Father, let us share the thrill of those two friends as we realise that Jesus really is alive. Amen.

Perhaps try...

- Spread ten or so items all over a table or on the floor.

- Blindfold one of your family, while the rest of you take one item away or add a new item. If this is too easy, you could just move one item to a different place.

- Take off the blindfold. Can you tell what we changed?

- If you can't do this activity, ask a quick question instead: Can you remember what it's like when you take a blindfold off?

- *Link: In today's story, it is as if Jesus takes the blindfold off his friends' eyes. They finally can see the surprise with their own eyes.*

This week's story

- *Where are we in the Bible?* Two of Jesus' friends have just had the world's most incredible Bible time with a total stranger as they walked along a road. They enjoyed it so much that they begged him to have a meal with them.

- *Look out for* that amazing moment when the two friends get the shock of their lives!

- *Read* the passage.

Luke 24 v 30-35

[30] *Jesus sat down with them and took some bread. He gave thanks for the food and divided it. Then he gave it to them.* [31] *And then, they were allowed to recognise Jesus. But when they saw who he was, he disappeared.*

[32] *They said to each other, "When Jesus talked to us on the road, it felt like a fire burning in us. It was exciting when he explained the true meaning of the Scriptures."*

[33] *So the two followers got up at once and went back to Jerusalem. There they found the 11 apostles and others gathered.* [34] *They were saying, "The Lord really has risen from death! He showed himself to Simon."*

[35] *Then the two followers told what had happened on the road. They talked about how they recognised Jesus when he divided the bread.*

Questions for us all

1. When did the two friends finally understand who the stranger was? Do you wonder why Jesus chose to show who he was during a meal?

2. When they realised it really was Jesus, what was the FIRST thing they wanted to talk about?

Question for 3s and 4s

What happened to Jesus as soon as they had understood who he was? That must have been a shock!

Question for 5-7s

Have you ever done something that makes your heart feel like it is on fire? You're so excited that you can hardly sit still. Which story in the Bible makes you most excited?

Question for over-7s

The friends were so excited about Jesus' Bible teaching that it felt like a fire burning in them. The Spirit's normal way of working today is to show us God speaking in the Bible. When we find the Bible a lot less than thrilling, what can we tell ourselves?

Question for teens

Do you believe that Jesus was clinically dead for days and then rose from the dead, never to die again? The question isn't about whether you have been told that. Do *you* believe in the resurrection?

Think and pray

Pray that more and more we would trust God to speak to us when we read the Bible. Pray about what you find difficult as you hear or read the Bible.

Got time to chat?

We believe in strange things. We believe that a dead man became alive again. We believe that a printed book has supernatural properties. We believe in life after death. We believe in a living all-powerful Lord who we cannot see.

Just so you know, everyone believes in strange things. They believe death is the end. They think the world and everything in it just happened, on its own. They think they can do whatever they like without consequences. These are strange things too!

Something more for the adults?

Has the Spirit been at work as you have looked at the Bible with your family? Have you got some stories and memories to tell others to encourage them?

Hit the Heart

DAY 32
All change!

Where are we going today?

When Jesus' friends were sure that he was risen from the dead, everything changed for them.

READY?

- Open your Bible to **Luke 24 v 30-34** (or read the passage from page 114).

LET'S GO!

Pray: Dear Father, thank you that Jesus is risen from the dead. Please show us the difference which that makes. Amen.

Perhaps try...

- **Optional.** Play a quick game of "It's Jesus!"

- All of you stand at one end of the room (Jerusalem). Choose one of you to be Jesus. You all walk slowly to the other end of the room (Emmaus). Unless you have a massive kitchen, keep the tiptoe steps tiny, so it takes a long time to get to the other end!

- When Jesus chooses, wherever you have got to, he says, "It's me, Jesus!" All the others then run back to where they came from (Jerusalem).

- If you can't do this activity, ask a quick question instead: What is the most exciting news you have ever heard?

- *Link: As soon as the two friends realised that their visitor was Jesus, they rushed all the way back to Jerusalem.*

This week's story

- *Where are we in the Bible?* There has been talk that Jesus has risen from the dead. The two friends on their way to Emmaus are not convinced. Then a stranger joins them on the walk to explain from the Bible that God's promised King had to die. Who is this stranger who can make sense of the whole Bible?

- *Look out for* the moment when they realise that it is Jesus—alive. What do you expect them to say immediately afterwards?

- *Read* the passage.

Luke 24 v 30-34

[30] *Jesus sat down with them and took some bread. He gave thanks for the food and divided it. Then he gave it to them.* [31] *And then, they were allowed to recognise Jesus. But when they saw who he was, he disappeared.*

[32] *They said to each other, "When Jesus talked to us on the road, it felt like a fire burning in us. It was exciting when he explained the true meaning of the Scriptures."*

[33] *So the two followers got up at once and went back to Jerusalem. There they found the 11 apostles and others gathered.* [34] *They were saying, "The Lord really has risen from death! He showed himself to Simon."*

Questions for us all

1. Where did the two friends go in such a rush?

2. What was their mood after they realised that Jesus was alive? What is *our* mood when we think about Jesus being alive?

Question for 3s and 4s

What did the two friends want to tell Jesus' disciples in Jerusalem?

Question for 5-7s

Imagine you are those two friends who have rushed to Jerusalem. Can you burst into the room and pretend *you* are telling Jesus' disciples in Jerusalem the news?

Question for over-7s

The two friends had spent the day walking away from Jerusalem sad, disappointed and confused. They finished the day by rushing back to Jerusalem. What do you think they would say has changed? Don't just say, "Jesus is alive!" That's too easy. What else has changed for these two friends? *(Their mood has changed. How? Their hopes have changed. How? Their thoughts have changed. How? Their plans have changed. How?)*

Question for teens

What event in human history has made the biggest change to humanity? The discovery of fire? The invention of the printing press? Walking on the moon? The end of a world war? How does Jesus' resurrection compare?

Think and pray

Thank God for the change that Jesus' resurrection makes to you. Does it change how you think about death? Or your priorities? Or just how you feel? Talk to God about some of these.

Got time to chat?

Try to spot a moment this week, in the life of your family, that could be changed by remembering that Jesus is not dead and buried but alive and ruling—on his throne, caring about your life, in charge of your life, wanting the whole of your life.

Something more for the adults?

Christ's resurrection often feels very distant. The immediate, dramatic change that those two friends experienced is rarely our daily experience. Read 2 Corinthians 4 v 16-18. Though our daily experience is of our bodies, which are aging, failing and wasting away, there will be a day when our bodies will be resurrected eternally, just as Jesus Christ's has been. That is the day we long for.

DAY 33
Come to the big party? No thanks!

Where are we going today?

Jesus taught that many say no to the greatest meal in heaven because they put themselves first.

READY?

- **Optional.** Find an envelope or just a folded piece of paper. Hide some treats around the room: some sweets, some snacks or a few favourite toys.

- Open your Bible to **Luke 14 v 15-20** (or read the passage from page 117).

LET'S GO!

Pray: Dear Father, please help us to understand the danger of not taking tight hold of the invitation to the greatest meal ever. Amen.

Perhaps try...

- Place the envelope in the middle of your family. Imagine that this is the invitation to the greatest meal ever. We're just waiting for the party to start.

- Around the room are hidden some treats. Let's go and find them.

- While they're looking, remove the invitation.

- If you can't do this activity, ask a quick question instead: Have you ever missed out on something spectacular?

- *Link: While the guests are waiting for the party to start, they get busy with other things that seemed so important. They miss out on being at the party.*

This week's story

- *Where are we in the Bible?* Jesus is still sitting at the meal with the religious leaders: the one that Jesus ruined! (See the picture on page 68.) Now, just as one of the guests changes the subject to talk about the great feast in heaven, Jesus makes it even more awkward by telling a story to show who will actually be there.

- *Look out for* the big shock in the story Jesus told.

- *Read* the passage.

Luke 14 v 15-20

 15 One of the men sitting at the table with Jesus heard these things. The man said to Jesus, "The people who will eat a meal in God's kingdom are blessed."

16 Jesus said to him, "A man gave a big banquet and invited many people. 17 When it was time to eat, the man sent his servant to tell the guests, 'Come! Everything is ready!'

18 "But all the guests said they could not come. Each man made an excuse. The first one said, 'I have just bought a field, and I must go look at it. Please excuse me.' 19 Another man said, 'I have just bought five pairs of oxen; I must go and try them. Please excuse me.' 20 A third man said, 'I just got married; I can't come.'"

Questions for us all

1. In the story, what was the servant's message for the invited guests?

2. And how many of these invited friends made it into the party?

Question for 3s and 4s

Look at the picture of the party (page 119). Can you see Jesus?
(Yes. He is in the middle.)

Can you see the people who were too busy to come?
(No! They were so busy that they missed the party!)

Question for 5-7s

Jesus told this story to show that some people say no to the greatest party in heaven. Can you act out what each person was doing when they were told the party was ready for them?

Question for over-7s

Imagine the moment when these three guests realised what they had missed out on. What do you think Jesus wants us to learn from their mistakes?

Question for teens

It sounds like a strange story. Getting married sounds like a good reason for missing a party. The other two have been interrupted right when they're in the middle of something important. And surely, if this banquet is a picture of heaven, no one would actually say no to heaven, would they? *(Jesus did choose important sounding reasons to get in the way of the party in heaven. We all fill our lives with activities that we think are important.)*

Think and pray

Younger children could thank God that there is definitely a great big party in heaven that everyone is invited to. Is there a warning that you hear in Jesus' story for yourself? Or are there people you love who you want to pray for?

Got time to chat?

As parents we can find it hard to ask our children blunt questions about whether they have said yes or no to Jesus' invitation and what they have decided about Jesus Christ. This might be a good time to ask them. You know your children. They trust you. Talk to them! Let them ask you questions.

Something more for the adults?

As you flick from Luke 13 v 22 to today's parable, you will see familiar passages and consistent themes. Lots of meals! The key contrast that Jesus presents is that of proud religious types vs. humble dependent types. We see that in today's parable. The three characters are proud. They want to manage their own time, they want to decide what is most important and there is an arrogance as if they are in charge of everything.

DAY 34

Come to the big party! What, me?

Where are we going today?

Jesus taught that the greatest meal in heaven will be full of shocked guests that God kindly brings in. They're sure they don't deserve it.

READY?

- Open your Bible to **Luke 14 v 21-24** (or read the passage from page 121).

LET'S GO!

Pray: Dear Father, thank you that there is a party in heaven to look forward to. Amen.

Perhaps try...

- **Optional.** Imagine that there is a party happening for only 20 people who will be hand-picked from all around the world. You have your chance right now to make sure you get to go to the party. What will you do or say to make sure you are chosen? One at a time. Go!

- Link: Yesterday we saw that some said they were too busy to come. Today we see that the people who get into the party are the ones who were sure it would NOT be them, who had never received an invitation.

This week's story

- *Where are we in the Bible?* Jesus is sitting with the religious leaders. One of the guests said that he can't wait to be in heaven, so Jesus told a story about the best party ever. You know the party he's talking about, don't you?

- *Look out for* who gets into this amazing party.

- *Read* the passage.

Luke 14 v 21-24

 21 [Jesus said,] "So the servant returned. He told his master what had happened. Then the master became angry and said, 'Go at once into the streets and alleys of the town. Bring in the poor, the crippled, the blind, and the lame.' 22 Later the servant said to him, 'Master, I did what you told me to do, but we still have places for more people.' 23 The master said to the servant, 'Go out to the roads and country lanes. Tell the people there to come. I want my house to be full! 24 None of those men that I invited first will ever eat with me!'"

Questions for us all

1. How did the master feel when all his guests were too busy to come to the party? Do you think God is like that?

2. How full is the party when the fun starts?

Question for 3s and 4s

Did you hear who got to go to the party?

Question for 5-7s

What do you think the poorest people said as they walked into the biggest, best banquet? What about the man without any legs? Or the lady who was blind and deaf?

Question for over-7s

If I was telling someone a story to help them understand who will be in heaven with Jesus for ever, it wouldn't have been like this! What is the biggest surprise in Jesus' story? What do you think he wants us to think about? *(Jesus wants us to be very careful that we don't start thinking we deserve to be in the party, or that we have done something clever to be there, or that Jesus is very lucky to have us at his party.)*

Question for teens

Things you don't expect to hear at a great party would include "Let's just eat some stale bread instead of cake", "I'm fine drinking lukewarm water" and "Not one of those who were invited will get a taste of my banquet". But Jesus really does have the host saying one of those in his story. It's bonkers! And yet, as we've seen at each dinner, Jesus always invited the worst, the most hated and the loneliest people to his parties. So why did he say this?

Think and pray

As you think about the great party in heaven, what would you like to say to the host? Do you want to say, "Thank you that Jesus has made it possible for me to go" or "Sorry that I forget that it's Jesus, not me, who will make sure I'm in the party"? Maybe you can say, "Please can you pull me into the party?"

Got time to chat?

We have sat with Jesus through amazing meals. But we finish with the most important one: the one we are invited to, which will last for ever. The obvious question to finish with is "Do you want to have a meal with Jesus?"

Something more for the adults?

Read Revelation 19 v 5-10. Welcome to the meal to which all others point. The final meal. No need to check your wardrobe for this one. You will be handed fine linen, bright and clean. All stains have been washed away by Christ. We have been invited to his wedding feast. Our Lord sits at the top table. And you and I are the bride. Dressed in pure white. He is waiting. Keep looking forward to that better meal.

Top tips

- A hardback Bible sits open, flat on a table, so it is one less thing to go wrong and it won't distract children by flicking shut. For under-11s, the International Children's Bible is a good, simplified version. This is the version we have printed in this book. Otherwise the New International Version is great. For a large family, each person will need their own Bible, using the same translation, or their own copy of this book. Alternatively, in whatever translation you choose, you could print out copies of the passage (from www.biblegateway.com).

- Under-5s will struggle with many of the activities. They find it hard to understand that a drama is recreating an ancient story. They find metaphors, illustrations and visual aids hard to process. This age-group would be helped by having a children's picture Bible to see what is happening in the Bible stories. The Beginners Bible and the Jesus Storybook Bible are good for this. These devotions will need to be kept very simple for them.

- Try to read through the devotion once, before you sit down with your children. Often, it will help if you grab a suggested object as a prop before you start. Occasionally, there is the option to prepare a visual aid.

- If your family are new to devotions, or if you are restarting them after a break and you face some opposition to the idea, you could set a ten-minute timer (and hide it, so that the ticking seconds aren't watched!). Promise that when the alarm goes off, you will stop the conversation and all present will pray in response. Keep that promise—no matter how far you've got.

- If your children are currently more malleable, then don't set a timer, as it may set an expectation that the ten minutes will be a form of torture.

- Do set an expectation that this time together will be the highlight of the day. Jesus talked about the Bible as "daily bread"—your family needs ten minutes like this each day to survive.

- Remember that there is huge value in your children seeing their parents answering questions from the Bible, talking about their faith, showing that they don't have all the answers and praying. It will have a lasting impact for children to see their parents engaging with the Bible, humbly accepting that they themselves are a work in progress and praying to their own Father in heaven.

- Many families are clinging on to sanity, joy, peace, hope or faith by their fingernails. Ask your children to help make these happen.

  - What time do we want these devotions to happen?

  - Where do we want them to happen so that they will be a great opportunity to concentrate and learn?

  - What will need to be done before we can sit down together each day?

  - What role can each of us play to make them happen?

  - Don't be disappointed if these devotions feel like ten minutes of slightly miserable chaos. If you can manage to do three or four so that there is a routine and a sense of expectation, then things will usually improve. As always with children, there will be days that leave you in despair. Those days will show you your need of Jesus Christ in your parenting. No bad thing.

- Change the plan if the plan isn't working.

- God bless you in this. Take a moment to pray for your efforts. If you don't already feel dependent on Jesus Christ in your parenting, you are about to!

Discover more of the wonder of the Easter story

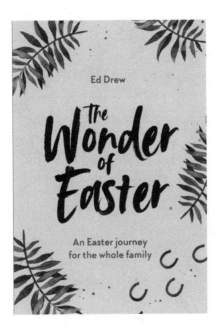

Take ten minutes a day to walk through Luke's Gospel and parts of the Old Testament with this flexible, easy-to-use Lent devotional. Differentiated questions for 3-4s, 5-7s, 7-12s, teens and adults allow both adults and children to celebrate the limitless wonder of Easter.

thegoodbook.com/wonder
thegoodbook.co.uk/wonder

Get your family excited about Christmas

These daily devotions in the Gospels give a thorough investigation of why Jesus came. In the lead-up to Christmas, families will explore 25 reasons why Jesus came, and they will see that what Jesus gives us is better than anything else we could wish for.

Each day there is a passage to read together, questions to think about, an explanation, and a prayer. There are also age-appropriate application questions, some for younger children and some for older children, as well as journalling space so that each family member can write or draw their own response to what God has shown them.

thegoodbook.com | thegoodbook.co.uk

faith in kids

exists to support churches and parents in raising children to trust in Jesus Christ eternally.

Point your kids in the right direction— when they're old they won't be lost.

Proverbs 22:6

Our simple, flexible resources enable churches and parents to confidently explore the Bible with children. Fun, relevant and truthful. Available from our website.

FOR CHURCHES: Sunday school & holiday club resources, school assembly scripts, training events

FOR PARENTS: Blog featuring articles, reviews, humour and resources

faithinkids.org

 faithinkids   faithinkids   FaithinKids

the good book

COMPANY

BIBLICAL | RELEVANT | ACCESSIBLE

At The Good Book Company, we are dedicated to helping Christians and local churches grow. We believe that God's growth process always starts with hearing clearly what he has said to us through his timeless word—the Bible.

Ever since we opened our doors in 1991, we have been striving to produce Bible-based resources that bring glory to God. We have grown to become an international provider of user-friendly resources to the Christian community, with believers of all backgrounds and denominations using our books, Bible studies,.devotionals, evangelistic resources, and DVD-based courses.

We want to equip ordinary Christians to live for Christ day by day, and churches to grow in their knowledge of God, their love for one another, and the effectiveness of their outreach.

Call us for a discussion of your needs or visit one of our local websites for more information on the resources and services we provide.

Your friends at The Good Book Company

thegoodbook.com | thegoodbook.co.uk
thegoodbook.com.au | thegoodbook.co.nz
thegoodbook.co.in